FAMOUS AFFINITIES OF HISTORY

THE ROMANCE OF DEVOTION

VOLUME IV OF IV.

LYNDON ORR

1st WORLD
LIBRARY
Literary Society

Famous Affinities of History, Vol 4

Lyndon Orr

© 1st World Library – Literary Society, 2004
PO Box 2211
Fairfield, IA 52556
www.1stworldlibrary.org
First Edition

LCCN: 2004195342

Softcover ISBN: 1-4218-0176-0
Hardcover ISBN: 1-4218-0076-4
eBook ISBN: 1-4218-0276-7

Purchase *"Famous Affinities of History Vol 4"*
as a traditional bound book at:
www.1stWorldLibrary.org/purchase.asp?ISBN=1-4218-0176-0

1st World Library Literary Society is a nonprofit
organization dedicated to promoting literacy by:

- Creating a free internet library accessible from any computer worldwide.
- Hosting writing competitions and offering book publishing scholarships.

Famous Affinities of History, Vol 4
contributed by Tim, Ed & Rodney
in support of
1st World Library Literary Society

CONTENTS

DEAN SWIFT AND THE TWO ESTHERS

The story of Jonathan Swift and of the two women who gave their lives for love of him is familiar to every student of English literature. Swift himself, both in letters and in politics, stands out a conspicuous figure in the reigns of King William III and Queen Anne. By writing Gulliver's Travels he made himself immortal. The external facts of his singular relations with two charming women are sufficiently well known; but a definite explanation of these facts has never yet been given. Swift held his tongue with a repellent taciturnity. No one ever dared to question him. Whether the true solution belongs to the sphere of psychology or of physiology is a question that remains unanswered.

But, as the case is one of the most puzzling in the annals of love, it may be well to set forth the circumstances very briefly, to weigh the theories that have already been advanced, and to suggest another.

Jonathan Swift was of Yorkshire stock, though happened to be born in Dublin, and thus is often spoken of as "the great Irish satirist," or "the Irish dean." It was, in truth, his fate to spend much of his life in Ireland, and to die there, near the cathedral where his remains now rest; but in truth he hated Ireland and everything connected with it, just as he hated Scotland and everything that was Scottish. He was an Englishman to the core.

High-stomached, proud, obstinate, and over-mastering, independence was the dream of his life. He would accept no favors, lest he should put himself under obligation; and although he could give generously, and even lavishly, he lived for the most part a miser's life, hoarding every penny and halfpenny that he could. Whatever one may think of him, there is no doubt that he was a very manly man. Too many of his portraits give the impression of a sour, supercilious pedant; but the finest of them all - that by Jervas - shows him as he must have been at his very prime, with a face that was almost handsome, and a look of attractive humor which strengthens rather than lessens the power of his brows and of the large, lambent eyes beneath them.

At fifteen he entered Trinity College, in Dublin, where he read widely but studied little, so that his degree was finally granted him only as a special favor. At twenty-one he first visited England, and became secretary to Sir William Temple, at Moor Park. Temple, after a distinguished career in diplomacy, had retired to his fine country estate in Surrey. He is remembered now for several things - for having entertained Peter the Great of Russia; for having, while young, won the affections of Dorothy Osborne, whose letters to him are charming in their grace and archness; for having been the patron of Jonathan Swift; and for fathering the young girl named Esther Johnson, a waif, born out of wedlock, to whom Temple gave a place in his household.

When Swift first met her, Esther Johnson was only eight years old; and part of his duties at Moor Park consisted in giving her what was then an unusual education for a girl. She was, however, still a child, and nothing serious could have passed between the raw youth and this little girl who learned the lessons that he imposed upon her.

Such acquaintance as they had was rudely broken off. Temple, a man of high position, treated Swift with an urbane condescension which drove the young man's independent soul into a frenzy. He returned to Ireland, where he was ordained a clergyman, and received a small parish at Kilroot, near Belfast.

It was here that the love-note was first seriously heard in the discordant music of Swift's career. A college friend of his named Waring had a sister who was about the age of Swift, and whom he met quite frequently at Kilroot. Not very much is known of this episode, but there is evidence that Swift fell in love with the girl, whom he rather romantically called "Varina."

This cannot be called a serious love-affair. Swift was lonely, and Jane Waring was probably the only girl of refinement who lived near Kilroot. Furthermore, she had inherited a small fortune, while Swift was miserably poor, and had nothing to offer except the shadowy prospect of future advancement in England. He was definitely refused by her; and it was this, perhaps, that led him to resolve on going back to England and making his peace with Sir William Temple.

On leaving, Swift wrote a passionate letter to Miss Waring - the only true love-letter that remains to us of their correspondence. He protests that he does not want Varina's fortune, and that he will wait until he is in a position to marry her on equal terms. There is a smoldering flame of jealousy running through the letter. Swift charges her with being cold, affected, and willing to flirt with persons who are quite beneath her.

Varina played no important part in Swift's larger life thereafter; but something must be said of this affair in order to show, first of all, that Swift's love for her was due only to proximity, and that when he ceased to feel it he could be not only hard, but harsh. His fiery spirit must have made a deep impression on Miss Waring; for though she at the time refused him, she afterward remembered him, and tried to renew their old relations. Indeed, no sooner had Swift been made rector of a larger parish, than Varina let him know that she had changed her mind, and was ready to marry him; but by this time Swift had lost all interest in her. He wrote an answer which even his truest admirers have called brutal.

"Yes," he said in substance, "I will marry you, though you have treated me vilely, and though you are living in a sort of social sink. I am still poor, though you probably think otherwise. However, I will marry you on certain conditions. First, you must be educated, so that you can entertain me. Next, you must put up with all my whims and likes and dislikes. Then you must live wherever I please. On these terms I will take you, without reference to your looks or to your income. As to the first, cleanliness is all that I require; as to the second, I only ask that it be enough."

Such a letter as this was like a blow from a bludgeon. The insolence, the contempt, and the hardness of it were such as no self-respecting woman could endure. It put an end to their acquaintance, as Swift undoubtedly intended it should do. He would have been less censurable had he struck Varina with his fist or kicked her.

The true reason for Swift's utter change of heart is found, no doubt, in the beginning of what was destined to be his long intimacy with Esther Johnson. When Swift left Sir William Temple's in a huff, Esther had been a mere schoolgirl. Now, on his return, she was fifteen years of age, and seemed older. She had blossomed out into a very comely girl, vivacious, clever, and physically well developed, with dark hair, sparkling eyes, and features that were unusually regular and lovely.

For three years the two were close friends and intimate associates, though it cannot he said that Swift ever made open love to her. To the outward eye they were no more than fellow workers. Yet love does not need the spoken word and the formal declaration to give it life and make it deep and strong. Esther Johnson, to whom Swift gave the pet name of "Stella," grew into the existence of this fiery, hold, and independent genius. All that he did she knew. She was his confidante. As to his writings, his hopes, and his enmities, she was the mistress of all his secrets. For her, at last, no other man existed.

On Sir William Temple's death, Esther John son came into a small fortune, though she now lost her home at Moor Park. Swift returned to Ireland, and soon afterward he invited Stella to join him there.

Swift was now thirty-four years of age, and Stella a very attractive girl of twenty. One might have expected that the two would marry, and yet they did not do so. Every precaution was taken to avoid anything like scandal. Stella was accompanied by a friend - a widow named Mrs. Dingley - without whose presence, or that of some third person, Swift never saw Esther Johnson. When Swift was absent, how ever, the two ladies occupied his apartments; and Stella became more than ever essential to his happiness.

When they were separated for any length of time Swift wrote to Stella in a sort of baby-talk, which they called "the little language." It was made up of curious abbreviations and childish words, growing more and more complicated as the years went on. It is interesting to think of this stern and often savage genius, who loved to hate, and whose hate was almost less terrible than his love, babbling and prattling in little half caressing sentences, as a mother might babble over her first child. Pedantic writers have professed to find in Swift's use of this "little language" the coming shadow of that insanity which struck him down in his old age.

As it is, these letters are among the curiosities of amatory correspondence. When Swift writes "oo" for "you," and "deelest" for "dearest," and "vely" for "very," there is no need of an interpreter; but "rettle" for "let ter," "dallars" for "girls," and "givar" for "devil," are at first rather difficult to guess. Then there is a system of abbreviating. "Md" means "my dear," "Ppt" means "poppet," and "Pdfr," with which Swift sometimes signed his epistles, "poor, dear, foolish rogue."

The letters reveal how very closely the two were bound together, yet still there was no talk of marriage. On one occasion, after they had been together for three years in Ireland, Stella might have married another man. This was a friend of Swift's, one Dr. Tisdall, who made energetic love to the sweet-faced English girl. Tisdall accused Swift of poisoning Stella's mind against him. Swift replied that such was not the case. He said that no feelings of his own would ever lead him to influence the girl if she preferred another.

It is quite sure, then, that Stella clung wholly to Swift, and cared nothing for the proffered love of any other man. Thus through the years the relations of the two remained unchanged, until in 1710 Swift left Ireland and appeared as a very brilliant figure in the London drawing-rooms of the great Tory leaders of the day.

He was now a man of mark, because of his ability as a controversialist. He had learned the manners of the world, and he carried him self with an air of power which impressed all those who met him. Among these persons was a Miss Hester - or Esther - Vanhomrigh, the daughter of a rather wealthy widow who was living in London at that time. Miss Vanhomrigh - a name which she and her mother pronounced "Vanmeury" - was then seventeen years of age, or twelve years younger than the patient Stella.

Esther Johnson, through her long acquaintance with Swift, and from his confidence in her, had come to treat him almost as an intellectual equal. She knew all his moods, some of which were very difficult, and she bore them all; though when he was most tyrannous she became only passive, waiting, with a woman's wisdom, for the tempest to blow over.

Miss Vanhomrigh, on the other hand, was one of those girls who, though they have high spirit, take an almost voluptuous delight in yielding to a spirit that is stronger still. This beautiful creature felt a positive fascination in Swift's presence and his imperious manner. When his eyes flashed, and his voice thundered out words of anger, she looked at him with adoration, and bowed in a sort of ecstasy before him. If he chose to accost a great lady with "Well, madam, are you as ill-natured and disagreeable as when I met you last?" Esther Vanhomrigh thrilled at the insolent audacity of the man. Her evident fondness for him exercised a seductive influence over Swift.

As the two were thrown more and more together, the girl lost all her self-control. Swift did not in any sense make love to her, though he gave her the somewhat fanciful name of "Vanessa"; but she, driven on by a high-strung, unbridled temperament, made open love to him. When he was about to return to Ireland, there came one startling moment when Vanessa flung herself into the arms of Swift, and amazed him by pouring out a torrent of passionate endearments.

Swift seems to have been surprised. He did what he could to quiet her. He told her that they were too unequal in years and fortune for anything but friendship, and he offered to give her as much friendship as she desired.

Doubtless he thought that, after returning to Ireland, he would not see Vanessa any more. In this, however, he was mistaken. An ardent girl, with a fortune of her own, was not to be kept from the man whom absence only made her love the more. In addition, Swift carried on his correspondence with her, which served to fan the flame and to increase the sway that Swift had already acquired.

Vanessa wrote, and with every letter she burned and

pined. Swift replied, and each reply enhanced her yearning for him. Ere long, Vanessa's mother died, and Vanessa herself hastened to Ireland and took up her residence near Dublin. There, for years, was enacted this tragic comedy - Esther Johnson was near Swift, and had all his confidence; Esther Vanhomrigh was kept apart from him, while still receiving missives from him, and, later, even visits.

It was at this time, after he had become dean of St. Patrick's Cathedral, in Dublin, that Swift was married to Esther Johnson - for it seems probable that the ceremony took place, though it was nothing more than a form. They still saw each other only in the presence of a third person. Nevertheless, some knowledge of their close relationship leaked out. Stella had been jealous of her rival during the years that Swift spent in London. Vanessa was now told that Swift was married to the other woman, or that she was his mistress. Writhing with jealousy, she wrote directly to Stella, and asked whether she was Dean Swift's wife. In answer Stella replied that she was, and then she sent Vanessa's letter to Swift himself.

All the fury of his nature was roused in him; and he was a man who could be very terrible when angry. He might have remembered the intense love which Vanessa bore for him, the humility with which she had accepted his conditions, and, finally, the loneliness of this girl.

But Swift was utterly unsparing. No gleam of pity entered his heart as he leaped upon a horse and galloped out to Marley Abbey, where she was living - "his prominent eyes arched by jet-black brows and glaring with the green fury of a cat's." Reaching the house, he dashed into it, with something awful in his looks, made his way to Vanessa, threw her letter down upon the table and, after giving her one frightful glare, turned on his heel, and in a moment more was galloping back to Dublin.

The girl fell to the floor in an agony of terror and remorse. She was taken to her room, and only three weeks afterward was carried forth, having died literally of a broken heart.

Five years later, Stella also died, withering away a sacrifice to what the world has called Swift's cruel heartlessness and egotism. His greatest public triumphs came to him in his final years of melancholy isolation; but in spite of the applause that greeted The Drapier Letters and Gulliver's Travels, he brooded morbidly over his past life. At last his powerful mind gave way, so that he died a victim to senile dementia. By his directions his body was interred in the same coffin with Stella's, in the cathedral of which he had been dean.

Such is the story of Dean Swift, and it has always suggested several curious questions. Why, if he loved Stella, did he not marry her long before? Why, when he married her, did he treat her still as if she were not his wife? Why did he allow Vanessa's love to run like a scarlet thread across the fabric of the other affection, which must have been so strong?

Many answers have been given to these questions. That which was formulated by Sir Walter Scott is a simple one, and has been generally accepted. Scott believed that Swift was physically incapacitated for marriage, and that he needed feminine sympathy, which he took where he could get it, without feeling bound to give anything in return.

If Scott's explanation be the true one, it still leaves Swift exposed to ignominy as a monster of ingratitude. Therefore, many of his biographers have sought other explanations. No one can palliate his conduct toward Vanessa; but Sir Leslie Stephen makes a plea for him with reference to Stella. Sir Leslie points out that until Swift became dean of St. Patrick's his income was far too small to marry on, and that after his brilliant but disappointing three years in London, when his prospects of advancement were ruined, he felt himself a broken man.

Furthermore, his health was always precarious, since he suffered from a distressing illness which attacked him at intervals, rendering him both deaf and giddy. The disease is now known as Meniere's disease, from its classification by the French physician, Meniere, in 1861. Swift felt that he lived in constant danger of some sudden stroke that would deprive him either of life or reason; and his ultimate insanity makes it appear that his forebodings were not wholly futile. Therefore, though he married Stella, he kept the marriage secret, thus leaving her free, in case of his demise, to marry as a maiden, and not to be regarded as a widow.

Sir Leslie offers the further plea that, after all, Stella's life was what she chose to make it. She enjoyed Swift's friendship, which she preferred to the love of any other man.

Another view is that of Dr. Richard Garnett, who has discussed the question with some subtlety. "Swift," says Dr. Garnett, "was by nature devoid of passion. He was fully capable of friendship, but not of love. The spiritual realm, whether of divine or earthly things, was a region closed to him, where he never set foot." On the side of friendship he must greatly have preferred Stella to Vanessa, and yet the latter assailed him on his weakest side - on the side of his love of imperious domination.

Vanessa hugged the fetters to which Stella merely submitted. Flattered to excess by her surrender, yet conscious of his obligations and his real preference, he could neither discard the one beauty nor desert the other.

Therefore, he temporized with both of them, and when the choice was forced upon him he madly struck down the woman for whom he cared the less.

One may accept Dr. Garnett's theory with a somewhat altered conclusion. It is not true, as a matter of recorded fact, that Swift was incapable of passion, for when a boy at college he was sought out by various young women, and he sought them out in turn. His fiery letter to Miss Waring points to the same conclusion. When Esther Johnson began to love him he was heart-free, yet unable, because of his straitened means, to marry. But Esther Johnson always appealed more to his reason, his friendship, and his comfort, than to his love, using the word in its material, physical sense. This love was stirred in him by Vanessa. Yet when he met Vanessa he had already gone too far with Esther Johnson to break the bond which had so long united them, nor could he think of a life without her, for she was to him his other self.

At the same time, his more romantic association with

Vanessa roused those instincts which he had scarcely known himself to be possessed of. His position was, therefore, most embarrassing. He hoped to end it when he left London and returned to Ireland; but fate was unkind to him in this, because Vanessa followed him. He lacked the will to be frank with her, and thus he stood a wretched, halting victim of his own dual nature.

He was a clergyman, and at heart religious. He had also a sense of honor, and both of these traits compelled him to remain true to Esther Johnson. The terrible outbreak which brought about Vanessa's death was probably the wild frenzy of a tortured soul. It recalls the picture of some fierce animal brought at last to bay, and venting its own anguish upon any object that is within reach of its fangs and claws.

No matter how the story may be told, it makes one shiver, for it is a tragedy in which the three participants all meet their doom - one crushed by a lightning-bolt of unreasoning anger, the other wasting away through hope deferred; while the man whom the world will always hold responsible was himself destined to end his years blind and sleepless, bequeathing his fortune to a madhouse, and saying, with his last muttered breath:

"I am a fool!"

PERCY BYSSHE SHELLEY AND MARY GODWIN

A great deal has been said and written in favor of early marriage; and, in a general way, early marriage may be an admirable thing. Young men and young women who have no special gift of imagination, and who have practically reached their full mental development at twenty-one or twenty-two - or earlier, even in their teens - may marry safely; because they are already what they will be. They are not going to experience any growth upward and outward. Passing years simply bring them more closely together, until they have settled down into a sort of domestic unity, by which they think alike, act alike, and even gradually come to look alike.

But early wedlock spells tragedy to the man or the woman of genius. In their teens they have only begun to grow. What they will be ten years hence, no one can prophesy. Therefore, to mate so early in life is to insure almost certain storm and stress, and, in the end, domestic wreckage.

As a rule, it is the man, and not the woman, who makes the false step; because it is the man who elects to marry when he is still very young. If he choose some ill-fitting, commonplace, and unresponsive nature to match his own, it is he who is bound in the course of time to learn his great mistake. When the splendid eagle shall have got his growth, and shall begin to soar up into the vault of heaven, the poor little barn-yard fowl that he once believed to be his equal seems very far away in everything. He discovers that she is quite unable to follow him in his towering flights.

The story of Percy Bysshe Shelley is a singular one. The circumstances of his early marriage were strange. The breaking of his marriage-bond was also strange. Shelley himself was an extraordinary creature. He was blamed a great deal in his lifetime for what he did, and since then some have echoed the reproach. Yet it would seem as if, at the very beginning of his life, he was put into a false position against his will. Because of this he was misunderstood until the end of his brief and brilliant and erratic career.

SHELLEY AND MARY GODWIN

In 1792 the French Revolution burst into flame, the mob of Paris stormed the Tuileries, the King of France was cast into a dungeon to await his execution, and the wild sons of anarchy flung their gauntlet of defiance into the face of Europe. In this tremendous year was born young Shelley; and perhaps his nature represented the spirit of the time.

Certainly, neither from his father nor from his mother did he derive that perpetual unrest and that frantic fondness for revolt which blazed out in the poet when he was still a boy. His father, Mr. Timothy Shelley, was a very usual, thick-headed, unromantic English squire. His mother - a woman of much beauty, but of no exceptional traits - was the daughter of another squire, and at the time of her marriage was simply one of ten thousand fresh-faced, pleasant-spoken English country girls. If we look for a strain of the romantic in Shelley's ancestry, we shall have to find it in the person of his grandfather, who was a very remarkable and powerful character.

This person, Bysshe Shelley by name, had in his youth been associated with some mystery. He was not born in England, but in America - and in those days the name "America" meant almost anything indefinite and peculiar. However this might be, Bysshe Shelley, though a scion of a good old English family, had wandered in strange lands, and it was whispered that he had seen strange sights and done strange things. According to one legend, he had been married in America, though no one knew whether his wife was white or black, or how he had got rid of her.

He might have remained in America all his life, had not a small inheritance fallen to his share. This brought him back to England, and he soon found that England was in reality the place to make his fortune. He was a man of magnificent physique. His rovings had given him ease and grace, and the power which comes from a wide experience of life. He could be extremely pleasing when he chose; and he soon won his way into the good graces of a rich heiress, whom he married.

With her wealth he became an important personage, and consorted with gentlemen and statesmen of influence, attaching himself particularly to the Duke of Northumberland, by whose influence he was made a baronet. When his rich wife died, Shelley married a still richer bride; and so this man, who started out as a mere adventurer without a shilling to his name, died in 1813, leaving more than a million dollars in cash, with lands whose rent-roll yielded a hundred thousand dollars every year.

If any touch of the romantic which we find in Shelley is a matter of heredity, we must trace it to this able, daring, restless, and magnificent old grandfather, who was the beau ideal of an English squire - the sort of squire who had added foreign graces to native sturdiness. But young Shelley, the future poet, seemed scarcely to be English at all. As a young boy he cared nothing for athletic sports. He was given to much reading. He thought a good deal about abstractions with which most schoolboys never concern themselves at all.

Consequently, both in private schools and afterward at Eton, he became a sort of rebel against authority. He resisted the fagging-system. He spoke contemptuously of physical prowess. He disliked anything that he was obliged to do, and he rushed eagerly into whatever was forbidden.

Finally, when he was sent to University College, Oxford, he broke all bounds. At a time when Tory England was aghast over the French Revolution and its results, Shelley talked of liberty and equality on all occasions. He made friends with an uncouth but able fellow student, who bore the remarkable name of Thomas Jefferson Hogg - a name that seems rampant with republicanism - and very soon he got himself expelled from the university for publishing a little tract of an infidel character called "A Defense of Atheism."

His expulsion for such a cause naturally shocked his father. It probably disturbed Shelley himself; but, after all, it gave him some satisfaction to be a martyr for the cause of free speech. He went to London with his friend Hogg, and took lodgings there. He read omnivorously - Hogg says as much as sixteen hours a day. He would walk through the most crowded streets poring over a volume, while holding another under one arm.

His mind was full of fancies. He had begun what was afterward called "his passion for reforming everything." He despised most of the laws of England. He thought its Parliament ridiculous. He hated its religion. He was particularly opposed to marriage. This last fact gives some point to the circumstances which almost immediately confronted him.

Shelley was now about nineteen years old - an age at which most English boys are emerging from the public schools, and are still in the hobbledehoy stage of their formation. In a way, he was quite far from boyish; yet in his knowledge of life he was little more than a mere child. He knew nothing thoroughly - much less the ways of men and women. He had no visible means of existence except a small allowance from his father. His four sisters, who were at a boarding-school on Clapham Common, used to save their pin-money and send it to their gifted brother so that he might not actually starve. These sisters he used to call upon from time to time, and through them he made the acquaintance of a sixteen-year-old girl named Harriet Westbrook.

Harriet Westbrook was the daughter of a black-visaged keeper of a coffee-house in Mount Street, called "Jew Westbrook," partly because of his complexion, and partly because of his ability to retain what he had made. He was, indeed, fairly well off, and had sent his younger daughter, Harriet, to the school where

Shelley's sisters studied.

Harriet Westbrook seems to have been a most precocious person. Any girl of sixteen is, of course, a great deal older and more mature than a youth of nineteen. In the present instance Harriet might have been Shelley's senior by five years. There is no doubt that she fell in love with him; but, having done so, she by no means acted in the shy and timid way that would have been most natural to a very young girl in her first love-affair. Having decided that she wanted him, she made up her mind to get Mm at any cost, and her audacity was equaled only by his simplicity. She was rather attractive in appearance, with abundant hair, a plump figure, and a pink-and-white complexion. This description makes of her a rather doll-like girl; but doll-like girls are just the sort to attract an inexperienced young man who has yet to learn that beauty and charm are quite distinct from prettiness, and infinitely superior to it.

In addition to her prettiness, Harriet Westbrook had a vivacious manner and talked quite pleasingly. She was likewise not a bad listener; and she would listen by the hour to Shelley in his rhapsodies about chemistry, poetry, the failure of Christianity, the national debt, and human liberty, all of which he jumbled up without much knowledge, but in a lyric strain of impassioned eagerness which would probably have made the multiplication-table thrilling.

For Shelley himself was a creature of extraordinary fascination, both then and afterward. There are no likenesses of him that do him justice, because they cannot convey that singular appeal which the man himself made to almost every one who met him.

The eminent painter, Mulready, once said that Shelley was too beautiful for portraiture; and yet the descriptions of him hardly seem to bear this out. He was quite tall and slender, but he stooped so much as to make him appear undersized. His head was very small-quite disproportionately so; but this was counteracted to the eye by his long and tumbled hair which, when excited, he would rub and twist in a thousand different directions until it was actually bushy. His eyes and mouth were his best features. The former were of a deep violet blue, and when Shelley felt deeply moved they seemed luminous with a wonderful and almost unearthly light. His mouth was finely chiseled, and might be regarded as representing perfection.

One great defect he had, and this might well have overbalanced his attractive face. The defect in question was his voice. One would have expected to hear from him melodious sounds, and vocal tones both rich and penetrating; but, as a matter of fact, his voice was shrill at the very best, and became actually discordant and peacock-like in moments of emotion.

Such, then, was Shelley, star-eyed, with the delicate complexion of a girl, wonderfully mobile in his features, yet speaking in a voice high pitched and almost raucous. For the rest, he arrayed himself with care and in expensive clothing, even though he took no thought of neatness, so that his garments were almost always rumpled and wrinkled from his frequent writhings on couches and on the floor. Shelley had a strange and almost primitive habit of rolling on the earth, and another of thrusting his tousled head close up to the hottest fire in the house, or of lying in the glaring sun when out of doors. It is related that he composed one of his finest poems - "The Cenci" - in Italy, while stretched out with face upturned to an almost tropical sun.

But such as he was, and though he was not yet famous, Harriet Westbrook, the rosy-faced schoolgirl, fell in love with him, and rather plainly let him know that she had done so. There are a thousand ways in which a woman can convey this information without doing anything un-maidenly; and of all these little arts Miss Westbrook was instinctively a mistress.

She played upon Shelley's feelings by telling him that her father was cruel to her, and that he contemplated actions still more cruel. There is something absurdly comical about the grievance which she brought to Shelley; but it is much more comical to note the tremendous seriousness with which he took it. He wrote to his friend Hogg:

Her father has persecuted her in a most horrible way, by endeavoring to compel her to go to school. She asked my advice; resistance was the answer. At the same time I essayed to mollify Mr. Westbrook, in vain! I advised her to resist. She wrote to say that resistance was useless, but that she would fly with me and throw herself on my protection.

Some letters that have recently come to light show that there was a dramatic scene between Harriet Westbrook and Shelley - a scene in the course of which she threw her arms about his neck and wept upon his shoulder. Here was a curious situation. Shelley was not at all in love with her. He had explicitly declared this only a short time before. Yet here was a pretty girl about to suffer the "horrible persecution" of being sent to school, and finding no alternative save to "throw herself on his protection" - in other words, to let him treat her as he would, and to become his mistress.

The absurdity of the situation makes one smile. Common sense should have led some one to box Harriet's ears and send her off to school without a moment's hesitation; while as for Shelley, he should have been told how ludicrous was the whole affair. But he was only nineteen, and she was only sixteen, and the crisis seemed portentous. Nothing could be more flattering to a young man's vanity than to have this girl cast herself upon him for protection. It did not really matter that he had not loved her hitherto, and that he was already half engaged to another Harriet - his cousin, Miss Grove. He could not stop and reason with himself. He must like a true knight rescue lovely girlhood from the horrors of a school!

It is not unlikely that this whole affair was partly managed or manipulated by the girl's father. Jew Westbrook knew that Shelley was related to rich and titled people, and that he was certain, if he lived, to become Sir Percy, and to be the heir of his grand-father's estates. Hence it may be that Harriet's queer conduct was not wholly of her own prompting.

In any case, however, it proved to be successful. Shelley's ardent and impulsive nature could not bear to see a girl in tears and appealing for his help. Hence, though in his heart she was very little to him, his romantic nature gave up for her sake the affection that he had felt for his cousin, his own disbelief in marriage, and finally the common sense which ought to have told him not to marry any one on two hundred pounds a year.

So the pair set off for Edinburgh by stagecoach. It was a weary and most uncomfortable journey. When they reached the Scottish capital, they were married by the Scottish law. Their money was all gone; but their landlord, with a jovial sympathy for romance, let them have a room, and treated them to a rather promiscuous wedding-banquet, in which every one in the house participated.

Such is the story of Shelley's marriage, contracted at nineteen with a girl of sixteen who most certainly lured him on against his own better judgment and in the absence of any actual love.

The girl whom he had taken to himself was a well-meaning little thing. She tried for a time to meet her husband's moods and to be a real companion to him. But what could one expect from such a union? Shelley's father withdrew the income which he had previously given. Jew Westbrook refused to contribute anything, hoping, probably, that this course would bring the Shelleys to the rescue. But as it was, the young pair drifted about from place to place, getting very precarious supplies, running deeper into debt each day, and finding less and less to admire in each other.

Shelley took to laudanum. Harriet dropped her abstruse studies, which she had taken up to please her husband, but which could only puzzle her small brain. She soon developed some of the unpleasant traits of the class to which she belonged. In this her sister Eliza - a hard and grasping middle-aged woman - had her share. She set Harriet against her husband, and made life less endurable for both. She was so much older than the pair that she came in and ruled their household like a typical stepmother.

A child was born, and Shelley very generously went through a second form of marriage, so as to comply with the English law; but by this time there was little hope of righting things again. Shelley was much offended because Harriet would not nurse the child. He believed her hard because she saw without emotion an operation performed upon the infant.

Finally, when Shelley at last came into a considerable sum of money, Harriet and Eliza made no pretense of caring for anything except the spending of it in "bonnet-shops" and on carriages and display. In time - that is to say, in three years after their marriage - Harriet left her husband and went to London and to Bath, prompted by her elder sister.

This proved to be the end of an unfortunate marriage. Word was brought to Shelley that his wife was no longer faithful to him. He, on his side, had carried on a semi-sentimental platonic correspondence with a schoolmistress, one Miss Hitchener. But until now his life had been one great mistake - a life of restlessness, of unsatisfied longing, of a desire that had no name. Then came the perhaps inevitable meeting with the one whom he should have met before.

Shelley had taken a great interest in William Godwin, the writer and radical philosopher. Godwin's household was a strange one. There was Fanny Imlay, a child born out of wedlock, the offspring of Gilbert Imlay, an American merchant, and of Mary Wollstonecraft, whom Godwin had subsequently married. There was also a singularly striking girl who then styled herself Mary Jane Clairmont, and who was afterward known as Claire Clairmont, she and her brother being the early children of Godwin's second wife.

One day in 1814, Shelley called on Godwin, and found there a beautiful young girl in her seventeenth year, "with shapely golden head, a face very pale and pure, a great forehead, earnest hazel eyes, and an expression at once of sensibility and firmness about her delicately curved lips." This was Mary Godwin - one who had inherited her mother's power of mind and likewise her grace and sweetness.

From the very moment of their meeting Shelley and this girl were fated to be joined together, and both of them were well aware of it. Each felt the other's presence exert a magnetic thrill. Each listened eagerly to what the other said. Each thought of nothing, and each cared for nothing, in the other's absence. It was a great compelling elemental force which drove the two together and bound them fast. Beside this marvelous experience, how pale and pitiful and paltry seemed the affectations of Harriet Westbrook!

In little more than a month from the time of their first meeting, Shelley and Mary Godwin and Miss Clairmont left Godwin's house at four o 'clock in the morning, and hurried across the Channel to Calais. They wandered almost like vagabonds across France, eating black bread and the coarsest fare, walking on the highways when they could not afford to ride, and putting up with every possible inconvenience. Yet it is worth noting that neither then nor at any other time did either Shelley or Mary regret what they had done. To the very end of the poet's brief career they were inseparable.

Later he was able to pension Harriet, who, being of a morbid disposition, ended her life by drowning - not, it may be said, because of grief for Shelley. It has been told that Fanny Imlay, Mary's sister, likewise committed suicide because Shelley did not care for her, but this has also been disproved. There was really nothing to mar the inner happiness of the poet and the woman who, at the very end, became his wife. Living, as they did, in Italy and Switzerland, they saw much of their own countrymen, such as Landor and Leigh Hunt and Byron, to whose fascinations poor Miss Clairmont yielded, and became the mother of the little girl Allegra.

But there could have been no truer union than this of Shelley's with the woman whom nature had intended for him. It was in his love-life, far more than in his poetry, that he attained completeness. When he died by drowning, in 1822, and his body was burned in the presence of Lord Byron, he was truly mourned by the one whom he had only lately made his wife. As a poet he never reached the same perfection; for his genius was fitful and uncertain, rare in its flights, and mingled always with that which disappoints.

As the lover and husband of Mary Godwin, there was nothing left to wish. In his verse, however, the truest word concerning him will always be that exquisite sentence of Matthew Arnold:

"A beautiful and ineffectual angel beating his luminous wings against the void in vain."

THE STORY OF THE CARLYLES

To most persons, Tennyson was a remote and romantic figure. His homes in the Isle of Wight and at Aldworth had a dignified seclusion about them which was very appropriate to so great a poet, and invested him with a certain awe through which the multitude rarely penetrated. As a matter of fact, however, he was an excellent companion, a ready talker, and gifted with so much wit that it is a pity that more of his sayings have not been preserved to us.

One of the best known is that which was drawn from him after he and a number of friends had been spending an hour in company with Mr. and Mrs. Carlyle. The two Carlyles were unfortunately at their worst, and gave a superb specimen of domestic "nagging." Each caught up whatever the other said, and either turned it into ridicule, or tried to make the author of it an object of contempt.

This was, of course, exceedingly uncomfortable for such strangers as were present, and it certainly gave no pleasure to their friends. On leaving the house, some one said to Tennyson:

"Isn't it a pity that such a couple ever married?"

"No, no," said Tennyson, with a sort of smile under his

rough beard. "It's much better that two people should be made unhappy than four."

The world has pretty nearly come around to the verdict of the poet laureate. It is not probable that Thomas Carlyle would have made any woman happy as his wife, or that Jane Baillie Welsh would have made any man happy as her husband.

This sort of speculation would never have occurred had not Mr. Froude, in the early eighties, given his story about the Carlyles to the world. Carlyle went to his grave, an old man, highly honored, and with no trail of gossip behind him. His wife had died some sixteen years before, leaving a brilliant memory. The books of Mr. Froude seemed for a moment to have desecrated the grave, and to have shed a sudden and sinister light upon those who could not make the least defense for themselves.

For a moment, Carlyle seemed to have been a monster of harshness, cruelty, and almost brutish feeling. On the other side, his wife took on the color of an evil-speaking, evil-thinking shrew, who tormented the life of her husband, and allowed herself to be possessed by some demon of unrest and discontent, such as few women of her station are ever known to suffer from.

Nor was it merely that the two were apparently ill-mated and unhappy with each other. There were hints and innuendos which looked toward some hidden cause for this unhappiness, and which aroused the curiosity of every one. That they might be clearer, Froude afterward wrote a book, bringing out more plainly - indeed, too plainly - his explanation of the Carlyle family skeleton. A multitude of documents then came from every quarter, and from almost every one who had known either of the Carlyles. Perhaps the result to-day has been more injurious to Froude than to the two Carlyles.

Many persons unjustly speak of Froude as having violated the confidence of his friends in publishing the letters of Mr. and Mrs. Carlyle. They take no heed of the fact that in doing this he was obeying Carlyle's express wishes, left behind in writing, and often urged on Froude while Carlyle was still alive. Whether or not Froude ought to have accepted such a trust, one may perhaps hesitate to decide. That he did so is probably because he felt that if he refused, Carlyle might commit the same duty to another, who would discharge it with less delicacy and less discretion.

As it is, the blame, if it rests upon any one, should rest upon Carlyle. He collected the letters. He wrote the lines which burn and scorch with self-reproach. It is he who pressed upon the reluctant Froude the duty of printing and publishing a series of documents which, for the most part, should never have been published at all, and which have done equal harm to Carlyle, to his wife, and to Froude himself.

Now that everything has been written that is likely to be written by those claiming to possess personal knowledge of the subject, let us take up the volumes, and likewise the scattered fragments, and seek to penetrate the mystery of the most ill-assorted couple known to modern literature.

It is not necessary to bring to light, and in regular order, the external history of Thomas Carlyle, or of Jane Baillie Welsh, who married him. There is an extraordinary amount of rather fanciful gossip about this marriage, and about the three persons who had to do with it.

Take first the principal figure, Thomas Carlyle. His life until that time had been a good deal more than the life of an ordinary country-man. Many persons represent him as a peasant; but he was descended from the ancient lords of a Scottish manor. There was something in his eye, and in the dominance of his nature, that made his lordly nature felt. Mr. Froude notes that Carlyle's hand was very small and unusually well shaped. Nor had his earliest appearance as a young man been commonplace, in spite of the fact that his parents were illiterate, so that his mother learned to read only after her sons had gone away to Edinburgh, in order that she might be able to enjoy their letters.

At that time in Scotland, as in Puritan New England, in each family the son who had the most notable "pairts" was sent to the university that he might become a clergyman. If there were a second son, he became an advocate or a doctor of medicine, while the sons of less distinction seldom went beyond the parish school, but settled down as farmers, horse-dealers, or whatever might happen to come their way.

In the case of Thomas Carlyle, nature marked him out for something brilliant, whatever that might be. His quick sensibility, the way in which he acquired every sort of learning, his command of logic, and, withal, his swift, unerring gift of language, made it certain from the very first that he must be sent to the university as soon as he had finished school, and could afford to go.

At Edinburgh, where he matriculated in his fourteenth

year, he astonished every one by the enormous extent of his reading, and by the firm hold he kept upon it. One hesitates to credit these so-called reminiscences which tell how he absorbed mountains of Greek and immense quantities of political economy and history and sociology and various forms of metaphysics, as every Scotsman is bound to do. That he read all night is a common story told of many a Scottish lad at college. We may believe, however, that Carlyle studied and read as most of his fellow students did, but far beyond them, in extent.

When he had completed about half of his divinity course, he assured himself that he was not intended for the life of a clergyman. One who reads his mocking sayings, or what seemed to be a clever string of jeers directed against religion, might well think that Carlyle was throughout his life an atheist, or an agnostic. He confessed to Irving that he did not believe in the Christian religion, and it was vain to hope that he ever would so believe.

Moreover, Carlyle had done something which was unusual at that time. He had taught in several local schools; but presently he came back to Edinburgh and openly made literature his profession. It was a daring thing to do; but Carlyle had unbounded confidence in himself - the confidence of a giant, striding forth into a forest, certain that he can make his way by sheer strength through the tangled meshes and the knotty branches that he knows will meet him and try to beat him back. Furthermore, he knew how to live on very little; he was unmarried; and he felt a certain ardor which beseemed his age and gifts.

Through the kindness of friends, he received some

commissions to write in various books of reference; and in 1824, when he was twenty-nine years of age, he published a translation of Legendre's Geometry. In the same year he published, in the London Magazine, his Life of Schiller, and also his translation of Goethe's Wilhelm Meister. This successful attack upon the London periodicals and reviews led to a certain complication with the other two characters in this story. It takes us to Jane Welsh, and also to Edward Irving.

Irving was three years older than Carlyle. The two men were friends, and both of them had been teaching in country schools, where both of them had come to know Miss Welsh. Irving's seniority gave him a certain prestige with the younger men, and naturally with Miss Welsh. He had won honors at the university, and now, as assistant to the famous Dr. Chalmers, he carried his silk robes in the jaunty fashion of one who has just ceased to be an undergraduate. While studying, he met Miss Welsh at Haddington, and there became her private instructor.

This girl was regarded in her native town as something of a personage. To read what has been written of her, one might suppose that she was almost a miracle of birth and breeding, and of intellect as well. As a matter of fact, in the little town of Haddington she was simply prima inter pares. Her father was the local doctor, and while she had a comfortable home, and doubtless a chaise at her disposal, she was very far from the "opulence" which Carlyle, looking up at her from his lowlier surroundings, was accustomed to ascribe to her. She was, no doubt, a very clever girl; and, judging from the portraits taken of her at about this time, she was an exceedingly pretty one, with beautiful eyes and an abundance of dark glossy hair.

Even then, however, Miss Welsh had traits which might have made it certain that she would be much more agreeable as a friend than as a wife. She had become an intellectuelle quite prematurely - at an age, in fact, when she might better have been thinking of other things than the inwardness of her soul, or the folly of religious belief.

Even as a young girl, she was beset by a desire to criticize and to ridicule almost everything and every one that she encountered. It was only when she met with something that she could not understand, or some one who could do what she could not, that she became comparatively humble. Unconsciously, her chief ambition was to be herself distinguished, and to marry some one who could be more distinguished still.

When she first met Edward Irving, she looked up to him as her superior in many ways. He was a striking figure in her small world. He was known in Edinburgh as likely to be a man of mark; and, of course, he had had a careful training in many subjects of which she, as yet, knew very little. Therefore, insensibly, she fell into a sort of admiration for Irving - an admiration which might have been transmuted into love. Irving, on his side, was taken by the young girl's beauty, her vivacity, and the keenness of her intellect. That he did not at once become her suitor is probably due to the fact that he had already engaged himself to a Miss Martin, of whom not much is known.

It was about this time, however, that Carlyle became acquainted with Miss Welsh. His abundant knowledge, his original and striking manner of commenting on it, his almost gigantic intellectual power, came to her as a revelation. Her studies with Irving were now interwoven with her admiration for Carlyle.

Since Irving was a clergyman, and Miss Welsh had not the slightest belief in any form of theology, there was comparatively little that they had in common. On the other hand, when she saw the profundities of Carlyle, she at once half feared, and was half fascinated. Let her speak to him on any subject, and he would at once thunder forth some striking truth, or it might be some puzzling paradox; but what he said could never fail to interest her and to make her think. He had, too, an infinite sense of humor, often whimsical and shot through with sarcasm.

It is no wonder that Miss Welsh was more and more infatuated with the nature of Carlyle. If it was her conscious wish to marry a man whom she could reverence as a master, where should she find him - in Irving or in Carlyle?

Irving was a dreamer, a man who, she came to see, was thoroughly one-sided, and whose interests lay in a different sphere from hers. Carlyle, on the other hand, had already reached out beyond the little Scottish capital, and had made his mark in the great world of London, where men like De Quincey and Jeffrey thought it worth their while to run a tilt with him. Then, too, there was the fascination of his talk, in which Jane Welsh found a perpetual source of interest:

The English have never had an artist, except in poetry; no musician; no painter. Purcell and Hogarth are not exceptions, or only such as confirm the rule.

Is the true Scotchman the peasant and yeoman - chiefly the former?

Every living man is a visible mystery; he walks between two eternities and two infinitudes. Were we not blind as molea we should value our humanity at infinity, and our rank, influence and so forth - the trappings of our humanity - at nothing. Say I am a man, and you say all. Whether king or tinker is a mere appendix.

Understanding is to reason as the talent of a beaver - which can build houses, and uses its tail for a trowel - to the genius of a prophet and poet. Reason is all but extinct in this age; it can never be altogether extinguished.

The devil has his elect.

Is anything more wonderful than another, if you consider it maturely? I have seen no men rise from the dead; I have seen some thousands rise from nothing. I have not force to fly into the sun, but I have force to lift my hand, which is equally strange.

Is not every thought properly an inspiration? Or how is one thing more inspired than another?

Examine by logic the import of thy life, and of all lives. What is it? A making of meal into manure, and of manure into meal. To the cui bono there is no answer from logic.

In many ways Jane Welsh found the difference of range between Carlyle and Irving. At one time, she asked Irving about some German works, and he was obliged to send her to Carlyle to solve her difficulties. Carlyle knew German almost as well as if he had been born in Dresden; and the full and almost overflowing way in which he answered her gave her another impression of his potency. Thus she weighed the two men who might become her lovers, and little by little she came to think of Irving as partly shallow and partly narrow-minded, while Carlyle loomed up more of a giant than before.

It is not probable that she was a woman who could love profoundly. She thought too much about herself. She was too critical. She had too intense an ambition for "showing off." I can imagine that in the end she made her choice quite coolly. She was flattered by Carlyle's strong preference for her. She was perhaps repelled by Irving's engagement to another woman; yet at the time few persons thought that she had chosen well.

Irving had now gone to London, and had become the pastor of the Caledonian chapel in Hatton Garden. Within a year, by the extraordinary power of his eloquence, which, was in a style peculiar to himself, he had transformed an obscure little chapel into one which was crowded by the rich and fashionable. His congregation built for him a handsome edifice on Regent Square, and he became the leader of a new cult, which looked to a second personal advent of Christ. He cared nothing for the charges of heresy which were brought against him; and when he was deposed his congregation followed him, and developed a new Christian order, known as Irvingism.

Jane Welsh, in her musings, might rightfully have compared the two men and the future which each could give her. Did she marry Irving, she was certain of a life of ease in London, and an association with men and women of fashion and celebrity, among whom she could show herself to be the gifted woman that she was. Did she marry Carlyle, she must go with him to a desolate, wind-beaten cottage, far away from any of the things she cared for, working almost as a housemaid, having no company save that of her husband, who was already a dyspeptic, and who was wont to speak of feeling as if a rat were tearing out his stomach.

Who would have said that in going with Carlyle she had made the better choice? Any one would have said it who knew the three - Irving, Carlyle, and Jane Welsh.

She had the penetration to be certain that whatever Irving might possess at present, it would be nothing in comparison to what Carlyle would have in the coming future. She understood the limitations of Irving, but to her keen mind the genius of Carlyle was unlimited; and she foresaw that, after he had toiled and striven, he would come into his great reward, which she would share. Irving might be the leader of a petty sect, but Carlyle would be a man whose name must become known throughout the world.

And so, in 1826, she had made her choice, and had become the bride of the rough-spoken, domineering Scotsman who had to face the world with nothing but his creative brain and his stubborn independence. She had put aside all immediate thought of London and its lures; she was going to cast in her lot with Carlyle's, largely as a matter of calculation, and believing that she had made the better choice.

She was twenty-six and Carlyle was thirty-two when, after a brief residence in Edinburgh, they went down to Craigenputtock. Froude has described this place as the dreariest spot in the British dominions:

The nearest cottage is more than a mile from it; the elevation, seven hundred feet above the sea, stunts the trees and limits the garden produce; the house is gaunt and hungry-looking. It stands, with the scanty fields attached, as an island in a sea of morass. The landscape is unredeemed by grace or grandeur - mere undulating hills of grass and heather, with peat bogs in the hollows between them.

Froude's grim description has been questioned by some; yet the actual pictures that have been drawn of the place in later years make it look bare, desolate, and uninviting. Mrs. Carlyle, who owned it as an inheritance from her father, saw the place for the first time in March, 1828. She settled there in May; but May, in the Scottish hills, is almost as repellent as winter. She herself shrank from the adventure which she had proposed. It was her husband's notion, and her own, that they should live there in practical solitude. He was to think and write, and make for himself a beginning of real fame; while she was to hover over him and watch his minor comforts.

It seemed to many of their friends that the project was quixotic to a degree. Mrs. Carlyle delicate health, her weak chest, and the beginning of a nervous disorder, made them think that she was unfit to dwell in so wild and bleak a solitude. They felt, too, that Carlyle was too much absorbed with his own thought to be trusted with the charge of a high-spirited woman.

However, the decision had been made, and the newly married couple went to Craigenputtock, with wagons that carried their household goods and those of Carlyle's brother, Alexander, who lived in a cottage near by. These were the two redeeming features of their lonely home - the presence of Alexander Carlyle, and the fact that, although they had no servants in the ordinary sense, there were several farmhands and a dairy-maid.

Before long there came a period of trouble, which is easily explained by what has been already said. Carlyle, thinking and writing some of the most beautiful things that he ever thought or wrote, could not make allowance for his wife's high spirit and physical weakness. She, on her side - nervous, fitful, and hard to please - thought herself a slave, the servant of a harsh and brutal master. She screamed at him when her nerves were too unstrung; and then, with a natural reaction, she called herself "a devil who could never be good enough for him." But most of her letters were harsh and filled with bitterness, and, no doubt, his conduct to her was at times no better than her own.

But it was at Craigenputtock that he really did lay fast and firm the road to fame. His wife's sharp tongue, and the gnawings of his own dyspepsia, were lived down with true Scottish grimness. It was here that he wrote some of his most penetrating and sympathetic essays, which were published by the leading reviews of England and Scotland. Here, too, he began to teach his countrymen the value of German literature.

The most remarkable of his productions was that strange work entitled Sartor Resartus (1834), an extraordinary mixture of the sublime and the grotesque. The book quivers and shakes with tragic pathos, with inward agonies, with solemn aspirations, and with riotous humor.

In 1834, after six years at Craigenputtock, the Carlyles moved to London, and took up their home in Cheyne Row, Chelsea, a far from fashionable retreat, but one in which the comforts of life could be more readily secured. It was there that Thomas Carlyle wrote what must seem to us the most vivid of all his books, the History of the French Revolution. For this he had read and thought for many years; parts of it he had written in essays, and parts of it he had jotted down in journals. But now it came forth, as some one has said, "a truth clad in hell-fire," swirling amid clouds and flames and mist, a most wonderful picture of the accumulated social and political falsehoods which preceded the revolution, and which were swept away by a nemesis that was the righteous judgment of God.

Carlyle never wrote so great a book as this. He had reached his middle style, having passed the clarity of his early writings, and not having yet reached the thunderous, strange-mouthed German expletives which marred his later work. In the French Revolution he bursts forth, here and there, into furious Gallic oaths and Gargantuan epithets; yet this apocalypse of France seems more true than his hero-worshiping of old Frederick of Prussia, or even of English Cromwell.

All these days Thomas Carlyle lived a life which was partly one of seclusion and partly one of pleasure. At all times he and his dark-haired wife had their own sets, and mingled with their own friends. Jane had no means of discovering just whether she would have been happier with Irving; for Irving died while she was still digging potatoes and complaining of her lot at Craigenputtock.

However this may be, the Carlyles, man and wife, lived an existence that was full of unhappiness and rancor. Jane Carlyle became an invalid, and sought to allay her nervous sufferings with strong tea and tobacco and morphin. When a nervous woman takes to morphin, it almost always means that she becomes intensely jealous; and so it was with Jane Carlyle.

A shivering, palpitating, fiercely loyal bit of humanity, she took it into her head that her husband was infatuated with Lady Ashburton, or that Lady Ashburton was infatuated with him. She took to spying on them, and at times, when her nerves were all a jangle, she would lie back in her armchair and yell with paroxysms of anger. On the other hand, Carlyle, eager to enjoy the world, sought relief from his household cares, and sometimes stole away after a fashion that was hardly guileless. He would leave false addresses at his house, and would dine at other places than he had announced.

In 1866 Jane Carlyle suddenly died; and somehow, then, the conscience of Thomas Carlyle became convinced that he had wronged the woman whom he had really loved. His last fifteen years were spent in wretchedness and despair. He felt that he had committed the unpardonable sin. He recalled with anguish every moment of their early life at Craigen-puttock - how she had toiled for him, and waited upon him, and made herself a slave; and how, later, she had given herself up entirely to him, while he had thoughtlessly received the sacrifice, and trampled on it as on a bed of flowers.

Of course, in all this he was intensely morbid, and the diary which he wrote was no more sane and wholesome than the screamings with which his wife had horrified her friends. But when he had grown to be a very old man, he came to feel that this was all a sort of penance, and that the selfishness of his past must be expiated in the future. Therefore, he gave his diary to his friend, the historian, Froude, and urged him to publish the letters and memorials of Jane Welsh Carlyle. Mr. Froude, with an eye to the reading world, readily did so, furnishing them with abundant footnotes, which made Carlyle appear to the world as more or less of a monster.

First, there was set forth the almost continual unhappiness of the pair. In the second place, by hint, by innuendo, and sometimes by explicit statement, there were given reasons to show why Carlyle made his wife unhappy. Of course, his gnawing dyspepsia, which she strove with all her might to drive away, was one of the first and greatest causes. But again another cause of discontent was stated in the implication that Carlyle, in his bursts of temper, actually abused his wife. In one passage there is a hint that certain blue marks upon her arm were bruises, the result of blows.

Most remarkable of all these accusations is that which has to do with the relations of Carlyle and Lady Ashburton. There is no doubt that Jane Carlyle disliked this brilliant woman, and came to have dark suspicions concerning her. At first, it was only a sort of social jealousy. Lady Ashburton was quite as clever a talker as Mrs. Carlyle, and she had a prestige which brought her more admiration.

Then, by degrees, as Jane Carlyle's mind began to

wane, she transferred her jealousy to her husband himself. She hated to be out-shone, and now, in some misguided fashion, it came into her head that Carlyle had surrendered to Lady Ashburton his own attention to his wife, and had fallen in love with her brilliant rival.

On one occasion, she declared that Lady Ashburton had thrown herself at Carlyle's feet, but that Carlyle had acted like a man of honor, while Lord Ashburton, knowing all the facts, had passed them over, and had retained his friendship with Carlyle.

Now, when Froude came to write My Relations with Carlyle, there were those who were very eager to furnish him with every sort of gossip. The greatest source of scandal upon which he drew was a woman named Geraldine Jewsbury, a curious neurotic creature, who had seen much of the late Mrs. Carlyle, but who had an almost morbid love of offensive tattle. Froude describes himself as a witness for six years, at Cheyne Row, "of the enactment of a tragedy as stern and real as the story of Oedipus." According to his own account:

I stood by, consenting to the slow martyrdom of a woman whom I have described as bright and sparkling and tender, and I uttered no word of remonstrance. I saw her involved in a perpetual blizzard, and did nothing to shelter her.

But it is not upon his own observations that Froude relies for his most sinister evidence against his friend. To him comes Miss Jewsbury with a lengthy tale to tell. It is well to know what Mrs. Carlyle thought of this lady. She wrote:

It is her besetting sin, and her trade of novelist has aggravated it - the desire of feeling and producing violent emotions. ... Geraldine has one besetting weakness; she is never happy unless she has a grande passion on hand.

There were strange manifestations on the part of Miss Jewsbury toward Mrs. Carlyle. At one time, when Mrs. Carlyle had shown some preference for another woman, it led to a wild outburst of what Miss Jewsbury herself called "tiger jealousy." There are many other instances of violent emotions in her letters to Mrs. Carlyle. They are often highly charged and erotic. It is unusual for a woman of thirty-two to write to a woman friend, who is forty-three years of age, in these words, which Miss Jewsbury used in writing to Mrs. Carlyle:

You are never out of my thoughts one hour together. I think of you much more than if you were my lover. I cannot express my feelings, even to you - vague, undefined yearnings to be yours in some way.

Mrs. Carlyle was accustomed, in private, to speak of Miss Jewsbury as "Miss Gooseberry," while Carlyle himself said that she was simply "a flimsy tatter of a creature." But it is on the testimony of this one woman, who was so morbid and excitable, that the most serious accusations against Carlyle rest. She knew that Froude was writing a volume about Mrs. Carlyle, and she rushed to him, eager to furnish any narratives, however strange, improbable, or salacious they might be.

Thus she is the sponsor of the Ashburton story, in which there is nothing whatsoever. Some of the letters which Lady Ashburton wrote Carlyle have been destroyed, but not before her husband had perused them. Another set of letters had never been read by Lord Ashburton at all, and they are still preserved - friendly, harmless, usual letters. Lord Ashburton always invited Carlyle to his house, and there is no reason to think that the Scottish philosopher wronged him.

There is much more to be said about the charge that Mrs. Carlyle suffered from personal abuse; yet when we examine the facts, the evidence resolves itself into practically nothing. That, in his self-absorption, he allowed her to Sending Completed Page, Please Wait ... overflowed toward a man who must have been a manly, loving lover. She calls him by the name by which he called her - a homely Scottish name.

GOODY, GOODY, DEAR GOODY:

You said you would weary, and I do hope in my heart you are wearying. It will be so sweet to make it all up to you in kisses when I return. You will take me and hear all my bits of experiences, and your heart will beat when you find how I have longed to return to you. Darling, dearest, loveliest, the Lord bless you! I think of you every hour, every moment. I love you and admire you, like - like anything. Oh, if I was there, I could put my arms so close about your neck, and hush you into the softest sleep you have had since I went away. Good night. Dream of me. I am ever YOUR OWN GOODY.

It seems most fitting to remember Thomas Carlyle as a man of strength, of honor, and of intellect; and his wife as one who was sorely tried, but who came out of her suffering into the arms of death, purified and calm and worthy to be remembered by her husband's side.

THE STORY OF THE HUGOS

Victor Hugo, after all criticisms have been made, stands as a literary colossus. He had imaginative power which makes his finest passages fairly crash upon the reader's brain like blasting thunderbolts. His novels, even when translated, are read and reread by people of every degree of education. There is something vast, something almost Titanic, about the grandeur and gorgeousness of his fancy. His prose resembles the sonorous blare of an immense military band. Readers of English care less for his poetry; yet in his verse one can find another phase of his intellect. He could write charmingly, in exquisite cadences, poems for lovers and for little children. His gifts were varied, and he knew thoroughly the life and thought of his own countrymen; and, therefore, in his later days he was almost deified by them.

At the same time, there were defects in his intellect and character which are perceptible in what he wrote, as well as in what he did. He had the Gallic wit in great measure, but he was absolutely devoid of any sense of humor. This is why, in both his prose and his poetry, his most tremendous pages often come perilously near to bombast; and this is why, again, as a man, his vanity was almost as great as his genius. He had good reason to be vain, and yet, if he had possessed a gleam of humor, he would never have allowed his egoism to make him arrogant. As it was, he felt himself exalted above other mortals. Whatever he did or said or wrote was right because he did it or said it or wrote it.

This often showed itself in rather whimsical ways. Thus, after he had published the first edition of his novel, The Man Who Laughs, an English gentleman called upon him, and, after some courteous compliments, suggested that in subsequent editions the name of an English peer who figures in the book should be changed from Tom Jim-Jack.

"For," said the Englishman, "Tom Jim-Jack is a name that could not possibly belong to an English noble, or, indeed, to any Englishman. The presence of it in your powerful story makes it seem to English readers a little grotesque."

Victor Hugo drew himself up with an air of high disdain.

"Who are you?" asked he.

"I am an Englishman," was the answer, "and naturally I know what names are possible in English."

Hugo drew himself up still higher, and on his face there was a smile of utter contempt.

"Yes," said he. "You are an Englishman; but I - I am Victor Hugo."

In another book Hugo had spoken of the Scottish bagpipes as "bugpipes." This gave some offense to his Scottish admirers. A great many persons told him that the word was "bagpipes," and not "bugpipes." But he replied with irritable obstinacy:

"I am Victor Hugo; and if I choose to write it 'bugpipes,' it IS 'bugpipes.' It is anything that I prefer to make it. It is so, because I call it so!"

So, Victor Hugo became a violent republican, because he did not wish France to be an empire or a kingdom, in which an emperor or a king would be his superior in rank. He always spoke of Napoleon III as "M. Bonaparte." He refused to call upon the gentle-mannered Emperor of Brazil, because he was an emperor; although Dom Pedro expressed an earnest desire to meet the poet.

When the German army was besieging Paris, Hugo proposed to fight a duel with the King of Prussia, and to have the result of it settle the war; "for," said he, "the King of Prussia is a great king, but I am Victor Hugo, the great poet. We are, therefore, equal."

In spite, however, of his ardent republicanism, he was very fond of speaking of his own noble descent. Again and again he styled himself "a peer of France;" and he and his family made frequent allusions to the knights and bishops and counselors of state with whom he claimed an ancestral relation. This was more than inconsistent. It was somewhat ludicrous; because Victor Hugo's ancestry was by no means noble. The Hugos of the fifteenth and sixteenth centuries were not in any way related to the poet's family, which was eminently honest and respectable, but by no means one of distinction. His grandfather was a carpenter. One of his aunts was the wife of a baker, another of a barber, while the third earned her living as a provincial dressmaker.

If the poet had been less vain and more sincerely democratic, he would have been proud to think that he sprang from good, sound, sturdy stock, and would have laughed at titles. As it was, he jeered at all pretensions of rank in other men, while he claimed for himself distinctions that were not really his. His father was a soldier who rose from the ranks until, under Napoleon, he reached the grade of general. His mother was the daughter of a ship owner in Nantes.

Victor Hugo was born in February, 1802, during the Napoleonic wars, and his early years were spent among the camps and within the sound of the cannon-thunder. It was fitting that he should have been born and reared in an age of upheaval, revolt, and battle. He was essentially the laureate of revolt; and in some of his novels - as in Ninety-Three - the drum and the trumpet roll and ring through every chapter.

The present paper has, of course, nothing to do with Hugo's public life; yet it is necessary to remember the complicated nature of the man - all his power, all his sweetness of disposition, and likewise all his vanity and his eccentricities. We must remember, also, that he was French, so that his story may be interpreted in the light of the French character.

At the age of fifteen he was domiciled in Paris, and though still a schoolboy and destined for the study of law, he dreamed only of poetry and of literature. He received honorable mention from the French Academy in 1817, and in the following year took prizes in a poetical competition. At seventeen he began the publication of a literary journal, which survived until 1821. His astonishing energy became evident in the many publications which he put forth in these boyish days. He began to become known. Although poetry, then as now, was not very profitable even when it was admired, one of his slender volumes brought him the sum of seven hundred francs, which seemed to him not only a fortune in itself, but the forerunner of still greater prosperity.

It was at this time, while still only twenty years of age, that he met a young girl of eighteen with whom he fell rather tempestuously in love. Her name was Adele Foucher, and she was the daughter of a clerk in the War Office. When one is very young and also a poet, it takes very little to feed the flame of passion. Victor Hugo was often a guest at the apartments of M. Foucher, where he was received by that gentleman and his family. French etiquette, of course, forbade any direct communication between the visitor and Adele. She was still a very young girl, and was supposed to take no share in the conversation. Therefore, while the others talked, she sat demurely by the fireside and sewed.

Her dark eyes and abundant hair, her grace of manner, and the picture which she made as the firelight played about her, kindled a flame in the susceptible heart of Victor Hugo. Though he could not speak to her, he at least could look at her; and, before long, his share in the conversation was very slight. This was set down, at first, to his absent-mindedness; but looks can be as eloquent as spoken words. Mme. Foucher, with a woman's keen intelligence, noted the adoring gaze of Victor Hugo as he silently watched her daughter. The young Adele herself was no less intuitive than her mother. It was very well understood, in the course of a few months, that Victor Hugo was in love with Adele Foucher.

Lyndon Orr

Her father and mother took counsel about the matter, and Hugo himself, in a burst of lyrical eloquence, confessed that he adored Adele and wished to marry her. Her parents naturally objected. The girl was but a child. She had no dowry, nor had Victor Hugo any settled income. They were not to think of marriage. But when did a common-sense decision, such as this, ever separate a man and a woman who have felt the thrill of first love! Victor Hugo was insistent. With his supreme self-confidence, he declared that he was bound to be successful, and that in a very short time he would be illustrious. Adele, on her side, created "an atmosphere" at home by weeping frequently, and by going about with hollow eyes and wistful looks.

The Foucher family removed from Paris to a country town. Victor Hugo immediately followed them. Fortunately for him, his poems had attracted the attention of Louis XVIII, who was flattered by some of the verses. He sent Hugo five hundred francs for an ode, and soon afterward settled upon him a pension of a thousand francs. Here at least was an income - a very small one, to be sure, but still an income. Perhaps Adele's father was impressed not so much by the actual money as by the evidence of the royal favor. At any rate, he withdrew his opposition, and the two young people were married in October, 1822 - both of them being under age, unformed, and immature.

Their story is another warning against too early marriage. It is true that they lived together until Mme. Hugo's death - a married life of forty-six years - yet their story presents phases which would have made this impossible had they not been French.

For a time, Hugo devoted all his energies to work. The

record of his steady upward progress is a part of the history of literature, and need not be repeated here. The poet and his wife were soon able to leave the latter's family abode, and to set up their own household god in a home which was their own. Around them there were gathered, in a sort of salon, all the best-known writers of the day - dramatists, critics, poets, and romancers. The Hugos knew everybody.

Unfortunately, one of their visitors cast into their new life a drop of corroding bitterness. This intruder was Charles Augustin Sainte-Beuve, a man two years younger than Victor Hugo, and one who blended learning, imagination, and a gift of critical analysis. Sainte-Beuve is to-day best remembered as a critic, and he was perhaps the greatest critic ever known in France. But in 1830 he was a slender, insinuating youth who cultivated a gift for sensuous and somewhat morbid poetry.

He had won Victor Hugo's friendship by writing an enthusiastic notice of Hugo's dramatic works. Hugo, in turn, styled Sainte-Beuve "an eagle," "a blazing star," and paid him other compliments no less gorgeous and Hugoesque. But in truth, if Sainte-Beuve frequented the Hugo salon, it was less because of his admiration for the poet than from his desire to win the love of the poet's wife.

It is quite impossible to say how far he attracted the serious attention of Adele Hugo. Sainte-Beuve represents a curious type, which is far more common in France and Italy than in the countries of the north. Human nature is not very different in cultivated circles anywhere. Man loves, and seeks to win the object of his love; or, as the old English proverb has it:

It's a man's part to try,
And a woman's to deny.

But only in the Latin countries do men who have tried make their attempts public, and seek to produce an impression that they have been successful, and that the woman has not denied. This sort of man, in English-speaking lands, is set down simply as a cad, and is excluded from people's houses; but in some other countries the thing is regarded with a certain amount of toleration. We see it in the two books written respectively by Alfred de Musset and George Sand. We have seen it still later in our own times, in that strange and half-repulsive story in which the Italian novelist and poet, Gabriele d'Annunzio, under a very thin disguise, revealed his relations with the famous actress, Eleanora Duse. Anglo-Saxons thrust such books aside with a feeling of disgust for the man who could so betray a sacred confidence and perhaps exaggerate a simple indiscretion into actual guilt. But it is not so in France and Italy. And this is precisely what Sainte-Beuve attempted.

Dr. George McLean Harper, in his lately published study of Sainte-Beuve, has summed the matter up admirably, in speaking of The Book of Love:

He had the vein of emotional self-disclosure, the vein of romantic or sentimental confession. This last was not a rich lode, and so he was at pains to charge it secretly with ore which he exhumed gloatingly, but which was really base metal. The impulse that led him along this false route was partly ambition, partly sensuality. Many a worse man would have been restrained by self-respect and good taste. And no man with a sense of honor would have permitted The Book of Love to see the light - a small collection of verses recording his passion for Mme. Hugo, and designed to implicate her.

He left two hundred and five printed copies of this book to be distributed after his death. A virulent enemy of Sainte-Beuve was not too expressive when he declared that its purpose was "to leave on the life of this woman the gleaming and slimy trace which the passage of a snail leaves on a rose." Abominable in either case, whether or not the implication was unfounded, Sainte-Beuve's numerous innuendoes in regard to Mme. Hugo are an indelible stain on his memory, and his infamy not only cost him his most precious friendships, but crippled him in every high endeavor.

How monstrous was this violation of both friendship and love may be seen in the following quotation from his writings:

In that inevitable hour, when the gloomy tempest and the jealous gulf shall roll over our heads, a sealed bottle, belched forth from the abyss, will render immortal our two names, their close alliance, and our double memory aspiring after union.

Whether or not Mme. Hugo's relations with Sainte-Beuve justified the latter even in thinking such thoughts as these, one need not inquire too minutely. Evidently, though, Victor Hugo could no longer be the friend of the man who almost openly boasted that he had dishonored him. There exist some sharp letters which passed between Hugo and Sainte-Beuve. Their intimacy was ended.

But there was something more serious than this. Sainte-Beuve had in fact succeeded in leaving a taint upon the name of Victor Hugo's wife. That Hugo did not repudiate her makes it fairly plain that she was innocent; yet a high-spirited, sensitive soul like Hugo's could never forget that in the world's eye she was compromised. The two still lived together as before; but now the poet felt himself released from the strict obligations of the marriage-bond.

It may perhaps be doubted whether he would in any case have remained faithful all his life. He was, as Mr. H.W. Wack well says, "a man of powerful sensations, physically as well as mentally. Hugo pursued every opportunity for new work, new sensations, fresh emotion. He desired to absorb as much on life's eager forward way as his great nature craved. His range in all things - mental, physical, and spiritual - was so far beyond the ordinary that the gage of average cannot be applied to him. The cavil of the moralist did not disturb him."

Hence, it is not improbable that Victor Hugo might have broken through the bonds of marital fidelity, even had Sainte-Beuve never written his abnormal poems; but certainly these poems hastened a result which may or may not have been otherwise inevitable. Hugo no longer turned wholly to the dark-haired, dark-eyed Adele as summing up for him the whole of woman-hood. A veil was drawn, as it were, from before his eyes, and he looked on other women and found them beautiful.

It was in 1833, soon after Hugo's play "Lucrece Borgia" had been accepted for production, that a lady called one morning at Hugo's house in the Place

Royale. She was then between twenty and thirty years of age, slight of figure, winsome in her bearing, and one who knew the arts which appeal to men. For she was no inexperienced ingenue. The name upon her visiting-card was "Mme. Drouet"; and by this name she had been known in Paris as a clever and somewhat gifted actress. Theophile Gautier, whose cult was the worship of physical beauty, wrote in almost lyric prose of her seductive charm.

At nineteen, after she had been cast upon the world, dowered with that terrible combination, poverty and beauty, she had lived openly with a sculptor named Pradier. This has a certain importance in the history of French art. Pradier had received a commission to execute a statue representing Strasburg - the statue which stands to-day in the Place de la Concorde, and which patriotic Frenchmen and Frenchwomen drape in mourning and half bury in immortelles, in memory of that city of Alsace which so long was French, but which to-day is German - one of Germany's great prizes taken in the war of 1870.

Five years before her meeting with Hugo, Pradier had rather brutally severed his connection with her, and she had accepted the protection of a Russian nobleman. At this time she was known by her real name - Julienne Josephine Gauvin; but having gone upon the stage, she assumed the appellation by which she was thereafter known, that of Juliette Drouet.

Her visit to Hugo was for the purpose of asking him to secure for her a part in his forth-coming play. The dramatist was willing, but unfortunately all the major characters had been provided for, and he was able to offer her only the minor one of the Princesse Negroni.

The charming deference with which she accepted the offered part attracted Hugo's attention. Such amiability is very rare in actresses who have had engagements at the best theaters. He resolved to see her again; and he did so, time after time, until he was thoroughly captivated by her.

She knew her value, and as yet was by no means infatuated with him. At first he was to her simply a means of getting on in her profession - simply another influential acquaintance. Yet she brought to bear upon him the arts at her command, her beauty and her sympathy, and, last of all, her passionate abandonment.

Hugo was overwhelmed by her. He found that she was in debt, and he managed to see that her debts were paid. He secured her other engagements at the theater, though she was less successful as an actress after she knew him. There came, for a time, a short break in their relations; for, partly out of need, she returned to her Russian nobleman, or at least admitted him to a menage a trois. Hugo underwent for a second time a great disillusionment. Nevertheless, he was not too proud to return to her and to beg her not to be unfaithful any more. Touched by his tears, and perhaps foreseeing his future fame, she gave her promise, and she kept it until her death, nearly half a century later.

Perhaps because she had deceived him once, Hugo never completely lost his prudence in his association with her. He was by no means lavish with money, and he installed her in a rather simple apartment only a short distance from his own home. He gave her an allowance that was relatively small, though later he provided for her amply in his will. But it was to her that he brought all his confidences, to her he entrusted all his interests. She became to him, thenceforth, much more than she appeared to the world at large; for she was his friend, and, as he said, his inspiration.

The fact of their intimate connection became gradually known through Paris. It was known even to Mme. Hugo; but she, remembering the affair of Sainte-Beuve, or knowing how difficult it is to check the will of a man like Hugo, made no sign, and even received Juliette Drouet in her own house and visited her in turn. When the poet's sons grew up to manhood, they, too, spent many hours with their father in the little salon of the former actress. It was a strange and, to an Anglo-Saxon mind, an almost impossible position; yet France forgives much to genius, and in time no one thought of commenting on Hugo's manner of life.

In 1851, when Napoleon III seized upon the government, and when Hugo was in danger of arrest, she assisted him to escape in disguise, and with a forged passport, across the Belgian frontier. During his long exile in Guernsey she lived in the same close relationship to him and to his family. Mme. Hugo died in 1868, having known for thirty-three years that she was only second in her husband's thoughts. Was she doing penance, or was she merely accepting the inevitable? In any case, her position was most pathetic, though she uttered no complaint.

A very curious and poignant picture of her just before her death has been given by the pen of a visitor in Guernsey. He had met Hugo and his sons; he had seen the great novelist eating enormous slices of roast beef and drinking great goblets of red wine at dinner, and he had also watched him early each morning, divested of all his clothing and splashing about in a bath-tub on the top of his house, in view of all the town. One evening he called and found only Mme. Hugo. She was reclining on a couch, and was evidently suffering great pain. Surprised, he asked where were her husband and her sons.

"Oh," she replied, "they've all gone to Mme. Drouet's to spend the evening and enjoy themselves. Go also; you'll not find it amusing here."

One ponders over this sad scene with conflicting thoughts. Was there really any truth in the story at which Sainte-Beuve more than hinted? If so, Adele Hugo was more than punished. The other woman had sinned far more; and yet she had never been Hugo's wife; and hence perhaps it was right that she should suffer less. Suffer she did; for after her devotion to Hugo had become sincere and deep, he betrayed her confidence by an intrigue with a girl who is spoken of as "Claire." The knowledge of it caused her infinite anguish, but it all came to an end; and she lived past her eightieth year, long after the death of Mme. Hugo. She died only a short time before the poet himself was laid to rest in Paris with magnificent obsequies which an emperor might have envied. In her old age, Juliette Drouet became very white and very wan; yet she never quite lost the charm with which, as a girl, she had won the heart of Hugo.

The story has many aspects. One may see in it a retribution, or one may see in it only the cruelty of life. Perhaps it is best regarded simply as a chapter in the strange life-histories of men of genius.

THE STORY OF GEORGE SAND

To the student of feminine psychology there is no more curious and complex problem than the one that meets us in the life of the gifted French writer best known to the world as George Sand.

To analyze this woman simply as a writer would in itself be a long, difficult task. She wrote voluminously, with a fluid rather than a fluent pen. She scandalized her contemporaries by her theories, and by the way in which she applied them in her novels. Her fiction made her, in the history of French literature, second only to Victor Hugo. She might even challenge Hugo, because where he depicts strange and monstrous figures, exaggerated beyond the limits of actual life, George Sand portrays living men and women, whose instincts and desires she understands, and whom she makes us see precisely as if we were admitted to their intimacy.

But George Sand puzzles us most by peculiarities which it is difficult for us to reconcile. She seemed to have no sense of chastity whatever; yet, on the other hand, she was not grossly sensual. She possessed the maternal instinct to a high degree, and liked better to be a mother than a mistress to the men whose love she sought. For she did seek men's love, frankly and shamelessly, only to tire of it. In many cases she seems to have been swayed by vanity, and by a love of conquest, rather than by passion. She had also a spiritual, imaginative side to her nature, and she could be a far better comrade than anything more intimate.

The name given to this strange genius at birth was Amantine Lucile Aurore Dupin. The circumstances of her ancestry and birth were quite unusual. Her father was a lieutenant in the French army. His grandmother had been the natural daughter of Marshal Saxe, who was himself the illegitimate son of Augustus the Strong of Poland and of the bewitching Countess of Konigsmarck. This was a curious pedigree. It meant strength of character, eroticism, stubbornness, imagination, courage, and recklessness.

Her father complicated the matter by marrying suddenly a Parisian of the lower classes, a bird-fancier named Sophie Delaborde. His daughter, who was born in 1804, used afterward to boast that on one side she was sprung from kings and nobles, while on the other she was a daughter of the people, able, therefore, to understand the sentiments of the aristocracy and of the children of the soil, or even of the gutter.

She was fond of telling, also, of the omen which attended on her birth. Her father and mother were at a country dance in the house of a fellow officer of Dupin's. Suddenly Mme. Dupin left the room. Nothing was thought of this, and the dance went on. In less than an hour, Dupin was called aside and told that his wife had just given birth to a child. It was the child's aunt who brought the news, with the joyous comment:

"She will be lucky, for she was born among the roses and to the sound of music."

This was at the time of the Napoleonic wars. Lieutenant Dupin was on the staff of Prince Murat, and little Aurore, as she was called, at the age of three accompanied the army, as did her mother. The child was adopted by one of those hard-fighting, veteran regiments. The rough old sergeants nursed her and petted her. Even the prince took notice of her; and to please him she wore the green uniform of a hussar.

But all this soon passed, and she was presently sent to live with her grandmother at the estate now intimately associated with her name - Nohant, in the valley of the Indre, in the midst of a rich country, a love for which she then drank in so deeply that nothing in her later life could lessen it. She was always the friend of the peasant and of the country-folk in general.

At Nohant she was given over to her grand-mother, to be reared in a strangely desultory sort of fashion, doing and reading and studying those things which could best develop her native gifts. Her father had great influence over her, teaching her a thousand things without seeming to teach her anything. Of him George Sand herself has written:

Character is a matter of heredity. If any one desires to know me, he must know my father.

Her father, however, was killed by a fall from a horse; and then the child grew up almost without any formal education. A tutor, who also managed the estate; believed with Rousseau that the young should be reared according to their own preferences. Therefore, Aurore read poems and childish stories; she gained a smattering of Latin, and she was devoted to music and the elements of natural science. For the rest of the time she rambled with the country children, learned their games, and became a sort of leader in everything they did.

Her only sorrow was the fact that her mother was excluded from Nohant. The aristocratic old grand-mother would not allow under her roof her son's low-born wife; but she was devoted to her little grandchild. The girl showed a wonderful degree of sensibility.

This life was adapted to her nature. She fed her imagination in a perfectly healthy fashion; and, living so much out of doors, she acquired that sound physique which she retained all through her life.

When she was thirteen, her grandmother sent the girl to a convent school in Paris. One might suppose that the sudden change from the open woods and fields to the primness of a religious home would have been a great shock to her, and that with her disposition she might have broken out into wild ways that would have shocked the nuns. But, here, as elsewhere, she showed her wonderful adaptability. It even seemed as if she were likely to become what the French call a devote. She gave herself up to mythical thoughts, and expressed a desire of taking the veil. Her confessor, however, was a keen student of human nature, and he perceived that she was too young to decide upon the renunciation of earthly things. Moreover, her grand-mother, who had no intention that Aurore should become a nun, hastened to Paris and carried her back to Nohant.

The girl was now sixteen, and her complicated nature began to make itself apparent. There was no one to control her, because her grandmother was confined to her own room. And so Aurore Dupin, now in superb health, rushed into every sort of diversion with all the zest of youth. She read voraciously - religion, poetry, philosophy. She was an excellent musician, playing the piano and the harp. Once, in a spirit of unconscious egotism, she wrote to her confessor:

Do you think that my philosophical studies are compatible with Christian humility?

The shrewd ecclesiastic answered, with a touch of wholesome irony:

I doubt, my daughter, whether your philosophical studies are profound enough to warrant intellectual pride.

This stung the girl, and led her to think a little less of her own abilities; but perhaps it made her books distasteful to her. For a while she seems to have almost forgotten her sex. She began to dress as a boy, and took to smoking large quantities of tobacco. Her natural brother, who was an officer in the army, came down to Nohant and taught her to ride - to ride like a boy, seated astride. She went about without any chaperon, and flirted with the young men of the neighborhood. The prim manners of the place made her subject to a certain amount of scandal, and the village priest chided her in language that was far from tactful. In return she refused any longer to attend his church.

Thus she was living when her grandmother died, in 1821, leaving to Aurore her entire fortune of five hundred thousand francs. As the girl was still but seventeen, she was placed under the guardianship of the nearest relative on her father's side - a gentleman of rank. When the will was read, Aurore's mother made a violent protest, and caused a most unpleasant scene.

"I am the natural guardian of my child," she cried. "No one can take away my rights!"

The young girl well understood that this was really the parting of the ways. If she turned toward her uncle, she would be forever classed among the aristocracy. If she chose her mother, who, though married, was essentially a grisette, then she must live with grisettes, and find her friends among the friends who visited her mother. She could not belong to both worlds. She must decide once for all whether she would be a woman of rank or a woman entirely separated from the circle that had been her father's.

One must respect the girl for making the choice she did. Understanding the situation absolutely, she chose her mother; and perhaps one would not have had her do otherwise. Yet in the long run it was bound to be a mistake. Aurore was clever, refined, well read, and had had the training of a fashionable convent school. The mother was ignorant and coarse, as was inevitable, with one who before her marriage had been half shop-girl and half courtesan. The two could not live long together, and hence it was not unnatural that Aurore Dupin should marry, to enter upon a new career.

Her fortune was a fairly large one for the times, and yet not large enough to attract men who were quite her equals. Presently, however, it brought to her a sort of country squire, named Casimir Dudevant. He was the illegitimate son of the Baron Dudevant. He had been in the army, and had studied law; but he possessed no intellectual tastes. He was outwardly eligible; but he was of a coarse type - a man who, with passing years, would be likely to take to drink and vicious amusements, and in serious life cared only for his cattle, his horses, and his hunting. He had, however, a sort of jollity about him which appealed to this girl of eighteen; and so a marriage was arranged. Aurore Dupin became his wife in 1822, and he secured the control of her fortune.

The first few years after her marriage were not unhappy. She had a son, Maurice Dudevant, and a daughter, Solange, and she loved them both. But it was impossible that she should continue vegetating mentally upon a farm with a husband who was a fool, a drunkard, and a miser. He deteriorated; his wife grew more and more clever. Dudevant resented this. It made him uncomfortable. Other persons spoke of her talk as brilliant. He bluntly told her that it was silly, and that she must stop it. When she did not stop it, he boxed her ears. This caused a breach between the pair which was never healed. Dudevant drank more and more heavily, and jeered at his wife because she was "always looking for noon at fourteen o'clock." He had always flirted with the country girls; but now he openly consorted with his wife's chambermaid.

Mme. Dudevant, on her side, would have nothing more to do with this rustic rake. She formed what she called a platonic friendship - and it was really so - with a certain M. de Seze, who was advocate-general at Bordeaux. With him this clever woman could talk without being called silly, and he took sincere pleasure in her company. He might, in fact, have gone much further, had not both of them been in an impossible situation.

Aurore Dudevant really believed that she was swayed by a pure and mystic passion. De Seze, on the other hand, believed this mystic passion to be genuine love. Coming to visit her at Nohant, he was revolted by the clownish husband with whom she lived. It gave him an esthetic shock to see that she had borne children to this boor. Therefore he shrank back from her, and in time their relation faded into nothingness.

It happened, soon after, that she found a packet in her husband's desk, marked "Not to be opened until after my death." She wrote of this in her correspondence:

I had not the patience to wait till widowhood. No one can be sure of surviving anybody. I assumed that my husband had died, and I was very glad to learn what he thought of me while he was alive. Since the package was addressed to me, it was not dishonorable for me to open it.

And so she opened it. It proved to be his will, but containing, as a preamble, his curses on her, expressions of contempt, and all the vulgar outpouring of an evil temper and angry passion. She went to her husband as he was opening a bottle, and flung the document upon the table. He cowered at her glance, at her firmness, and at her cold hatred. He grumbled and argued and entreated; but all that his wife would say in answer was:

"I must have an allowance. I am going to Paris, and my children are to remain here."

At last he yielded, and she went at once to Paris, taking her daughter with her, and having the promise of fifteen hundred francs a year out of the half-million that was hers by right.

In Paris she developed into a thorough-paced Bohemian. She tried to make a living in sundry hopeless ways, and at last she took to literature. She was living in a garret, with little to eat, and sometimes without a fire in winter. She had some friends who helped her as well as they could, but though she was attached to the Figaro, her earnings for the first month amounted to only fifteen francs.

Nevertheless, she would not despair. The editors and publishers might turn the cold shoulder to her, but she would not give up her ambitions. She went down into the Latin Quarter, and there shook off the proprieties of life. She assumed the garb of a man, and with her quick perception she came to know the left bank of the Seine just as she had known the country-side at Nohant or the little world at her convent school. She never expected again to see any woman of her own rank in life. Her mother's influence became strong in her. She wrote:

The proprieties are the guiding principle of people without soul and virtue. The good opinion of the world is a prostitute who gives herself to the highest bidder.

She still pursued her trade of journalism, calling herself a "newspaper mechanic," sitting all day in the office of the Figaro and writing whatever was demanded, while at night she would prowl in the streets haunting the cafes, continuing to dress like a man, drinking sour wine, and smoking cheap cigars.

One of her companions in this sort of hand-to-mouth journalism was a young student and writer named Jules

Sandeau, a man seven years younger than his comrade. He was at that time as indigent as she, and their hardships, shared in common, brought them very close together. He was clever, boyish, and sensitive, and it was not long before he had fallen at her feet and kissed her knees, begging that she would requite the love he felt for her. According to herself, she resisted him for six months, and then at last she yielded. The two made their home together, and for a while were wonderfully happy. Their work and their diversions they enjoyed in common, and now for the first time she experienced emotions which in all probability she had never known before.

Probably not very much importance is to be given to the earlier flirtations of George Sand, though she herself never tried to stop the mouth of scandal. Even before she left her husband, she was credited with having four lovers; but all she said, when the report was brought to her, was this: "Four lovers are none too many for one with such lively passions as mine."

This very frankness makes it likely that she enjoyed shocking her prim neighbors at Nohant. But if she only played at love-making then, she now gave herself up to it with entire abandonment, intoxicated, fascinated, satisfied. She herself wrote:

How I wish I could impart to you this sense of the intensity and joyousness of life that I have in my veins. To live! How sweet it is, and how good, in spite of annoyances, husbands, debts, relations, scandal-mongers, sufferings, and irritations! To live! It is intoxicating! To love, and to be loved! It is happiness! It is heaven!

In collaboration with Jules Sandeau, she wrote a novel called Rose et Blanche. The two lovers were uncertain what name to place upon the title-page, but finally they hit upon the pseudonym of Jules Sand. The book succeeded; but thereafter each of them wrote separately, Jules Sandeau using his own name, and Mme. Dudevant styling herself George Sand, a name by which she was to be illustrious ever after.

As a novelist, she had found her real vocation. She was not yet well known, but she was on the verge of fame. As soon as she had written Indiana and Valentine, George Sand had secured a place in the world of letters. The magazine which still exists as the Revue des Deux Mondes gave her a retaining fee of four thousand francs a year, and many other publications begged her to write serial stories for them.

The vein which ran through all her stories was new and piquant. As was said of her:

In George Sand, whenever a lady wishes to change her lover, God is always there to make the transfer easy.

In other words, she preached free love in the name of religion. This was not a new doctrine with her. After the first break with her husband, she had made up her mind about certain matters, and wrote:

One is no more justified in claiming the ownership of a soul than in claiming the ownership of a slave.

According to her, the ties between a man and a woman are sacred only when they are sanctified by love; and she distinguished between love and passion in this epigram:

Love seeks to give, while passion seeks to take.

At this time, George Sand was in her twenty-seventh year. She was not beautiful, though there was something about her which attracted observation. Of middle height, she was fairly slender. Her eyes were somewhat projecting, and her mouth was almost sullen when in repose. Her manners were peculiar, combining boldness with timidity. Her address was almost as familiar as a man's, so that it was easy to be acquainted with her; yet a certain haughtiness and a touch of aristocratic pride made it plain that she had drawn a line which none must pass without her wish. When she was deeply stirred, however, she burst forth into an extraordinary vivacity, showing a nature richly endowed and eager to yield its treasures.

The existence which she now led was a curious one. She still visited her husband at Nohant, so that she might see her son, and sometimes, when M. Dudevant came to town, he called upon her in the apartments which she shared with Jules Sandeau. He had accepted the situation, and with his crudeness and lack of feeling he seemed to think it, if not natural, at least diverting. At any rate, so long as he could retain her half-million francs, he was not the man to make trouble about his former wife's arrangements.

Meanwhile, there began to be perceptible the very slightest rift within the lute of her romance. Was her love for Sandeau really love, or was it only passion? In his absence, at any rate, the old obsession still continued. Here we see, first of all, intense pleasure shading off into a sort of maternal fondness. She sends Sandeau adoring letters. She is afraid that his delicate appetite is not properly satisfied.

Yet, again, there are times when she feels that he is irritating and ill. Those who knew them said that her nature was too passionate and her love was too exacting for him. One of her letters seems to make this plain. She writes that she feels uneasy, and even frightfully remorseful, at seeing Sandeau "pine away." She knows, she avows, that she is killing him, that her caresses are a poison, and her love a consuming fire.

It is an appalling thought, and Jules will not understand it. He laughs at it; and when, in the midst of his transports of delight, the idea comes to me and makes my blood run cold, he tells me that here is the death that he would like to die. At such moments he promises whatever I make him promise.

This letter throws a clear light upon the nature of George Sand's temperament. It will be found all through her career, not only that she sought to inspire passion, but that she strove to gratify it after fashions of her own. One little passage from a description of her written by the younger Dumas will perhaps make this phase of her character more intelligible, without going further than is strictly necessary:

Mme. Sand has little hands without any bones, soft and plump. She is by destiny a woman of excessive curiosity, always disappointed, always deceived in her incessant investigation, but she is not fundamentally ardent. In vain would she like to be so, but she does not find it possible. Her physical nature utterly refuses.

The reader will find in all that has now been said the true explanation of George Sand. Abounding with life, but incapable of long stretches of ardent love, she became a woman who sought conquests everywhere without giving in return more than her temperament made it possible for her to do. She loved Sandeau as much as she ever loved any man; and yet she left him with a sense that she had never become wholly his. Perhaps this is the reason why their romance came to an end abruptly, and not altogether fittingly.

She had been spending a short time at Nohant, and came to Paris without announcement. She intended to surprise her lover, and she surely did so. She found him in the apartment that had been theirs, with his arms about an attractive laundry-girl. Thus closed what was probably the only true romance in the life of George Sand. Afterward she had many lovers, but to no one did she so nearly become a true mate.

As it was, she ended her association with Sandeau, and each pursued a separate path to fame. Sandeau afterward became a well-known novelist and dramatist. He was, in fact, the first writer of fiction who was admitted to the French Academy. The woman to whom he had been unfaithful became greater still, because her fame was not only national, but cosmopolitan.

For a time after her deception by Sandeau, she felt absolutely devoid of all emotions. She shunned men, and sought the friendship of Marie Dorval, a clever actress who was destined afterward to break the heart of Alfred de Vigny. The two went into the country; and there George Sand wrote hour after hour, sitting by her fireside, and showing herself a tender mother to her little daughter Solange.

This life lasted for a while, but it was not the sort of life that would now content her. She had many visitors from Paris, among them Sainte-Beuve, the critic, who brought with him Prosper Merimee, then unknown, but later famous as master of revels to the third Napoleon and as the author of Carmen. Merimee had a certain fascination of manner, and the predatory instincts of George Sand were again aroused. One day, when she felt bored and desperate, Merimee paid his court to her, and she listened to him. This is one of the most remarkable of her intimacies, since it began, continued, and ended all in the space of a single week. When Merimee left Nohant, he was destined never again to see George Sand, except long afterward at a dinner-party, where the two stared at each other sharply, but did not speak. This affair, however, made it plain that she could not long remain at Nohant, and that she pined for Paris.

Returning thither, she is said to have set her cap at Victor Hugo, who was, however, too much in love with himself to care for any one, especially a woman who was his literary rival. She is said for a time to have been allied with Gustave Planche, a dramatic critic; but she always denied this, and her denial may be taken as quite truthful. Soon, however, she was to begin an episode which has been more famous than any other in her curious history, for she met Alfred de Musset, then a youth of twenty-three, but already well known for his poems and his plays.

Musset was of noble birth. He would probably have been better for a plebeian strain, since there was in him a touch of the degenerate. His mother's father had published a humanitarian poem on cats. His great-uncle had written a peculiar novel. Young Alfred was nervous, delicate, slightly epileptic, and it is certain that he was given to dissipation, which so far had affected his health only by making him hysterical. He was an exceedingly handsome youth, with exquisite manners, "dreamy rather than dazzling eyes, dilated nostrils, and vermilion lips half opened." Such was he when George Sand, then seven years his senior, met him.

There is something which, to the Anglo-Saxon mind, seems far more absurd than pathetic about the events which presently took place. A woman like George Sand at thirty was practically twice the age of this nervous boy of twenty-three, who had as yet seen little of the world. At first she seemed to realize the fact herself; but her vanity led her to begin an intrigue, which must have been almost wholly without excitement on her part, but which to him, for a time, was everything in the world.

Experimenting, as usual, after the fashion described by Dumas, she went with De Musset for a "honeymoon" to Fontainebleau. But they could not stay there forever, and presently they decided upon a journey to Italy. Before they went, however, they thought it necessary to get formal permission from Alfred's mother!

Naturally enough, Mme. de Musset refused consent. She had read George Sand's romances, and had asked scornfully:

"Has the woman never in her life met a gentleman?"

She accepted the relations between them, but that she should be asked to sanction this sort of affair was rather too much, even for a French mother who has become accustomed to many strange things. Then there was a curious happening. At nine o'clock at night, George Sand took a cab and drove to the house of Mme. de Musset, to whom she sent up a message that a lady wished to see her. Mme. de Musset came down, and, finding a woman alone in a carriage, she entered it. Then George Sand burst forth in a torrent of sentimental eloquence. She overpowered her lover's mother, promised to take great care of the delicate youth, and finally drove away to meet Alfred at the coach-yard.

They started off in the mist, their coach being the thirteenth to leave the yard; but the two lovers were in a merry mood, and enjoyed themselves all the way from Paris to Marseilles. By steamer they went to Leghorn; and finally, in January, 1834, they took an apartment in a hotel at Venice. What had happened that their arrival in Venice should be the beginning of a quarrel, no one knows. George Sand has told the story, and Paul de Musset - Alfred's brother - has told the story, but each of them has doubtless omitted a large part of the truth.

It is likely that on their long journey each had learned too much of the other. Thus, Paul de Musset says that George Sand made herself outrageous by her conversation, telling every one of her mother's adventures in the army of Italy, including her relations with the general-in-chief. She also declared that she herself was born within a month of her parents' wedding-day. Very likely she did say all these things, whether they were true or not. She had set herself to wage war against conventional society, and she did everything to shock it.

On the other hand, Alfred de Musset fell ill after having lost ten thousand francs in a gambling-house. George Sand was not fond of persons who were ill.

She herself was working like a horse, writing from eight to thirteen hours a day. When Musset collapsed she sent for a handsome young Italian doctor named Pagello, with whom she had struck up a casual acquaintance. He finally cured Musset, but he also cured George Sand of any love for Musset.

Before long she and Pagello were on their way back to Paris, leaving the poor, fevered, whimpering poet to bite his nails and think unutterable things. But he ought to have known George Sand. After that, everybody knew her. They knew just how much she cared when she professed to care, and when she acted as she acted with Pagello no earlier lover had any one but himself to blame.

Only sentimentalists can take this story seriously. To them it has a sort of morbid interest. They like to picture Musset raving and shouting in his delirium, and then, to read how George Sand sat on Pagello's knees, kissing him and drinking out of the same cup. But to the healthy mind the whole story is repulsive - from George Sand's appeal to Mme. de Musset down to the very end, when Pagello came to Paris, where his broken French excited a polite ridicule.

There was a touch of genuine sentiment about the affair with Jules Sandeau; but after that, one can only see in George Sand a half-libidinous grisette, such as her mother was before her, with a perfect willingness to experiment in every form of lawless love. As for Musset, whose heart she was supposed to have broken, within a year he was dangling after the famous singer, Mme. Malibran, and writing poems to her which advertised their intrigue.

After this episode with Pagello, it cannot be said that the life of George Sand was edifying in any respect, because no one can assume that she was sincere. She had loved Jules Sandeau as much as she could love any one, but all the rest of her intrigues and affinities were in the nature of experiments. She even took back Alfred de Musset, although they could never again regard each other without suspicion. George Sand cut off all her hair and gave it to Musset, so eager was she to keep him as a matter of conquest; but he was tired of her, and even this theatrical trick was of no avail.

She proceeded to other less known and less humiliating adventures. She tried to fascinate the artist Delacroix. She set her cap at Franz Liszt, who rather astonished her by saying that only God was worthy to be loved. She expressed a yearning for the affections of the elder Dumas; but that good-natured giant laughed at her, and in fact gave her some sound advice, and let her smoke unsentimentally in his study. She was a good deal taken with a noisy demagogue named Michel, a lawyer at Bourges, who on one occasion shut her up in her room and harangued her on sociology until she was as weary of his talk as of his wooden shoes, his shapeless greatcoat, his spectacles, and his skull-cap, Balzac felt her fascination, but cared nothing for her, since his love was given to Mme. Hanska.

In the meanwhile, she was paying visits to her husband at Nohant, where she wrangled with him over money matters, and where he would once have shot her had the guests present not interfered. She secured her dowry by litigation, so that she was well off, even without her literary earnings. These were by no means so large as one would think from her popularity and from the number of books she wrote. It is estimated that her whole gains amounted to about a million francs, extending over a period of forty-five years. It is just half the amount that Trollope earned in about the same period, and justifies his remark - "adequate, but not splendid."

One of those brief and strange intimacies that marked the career of George Sand came about in a curious way. Octave Feuillet, a man of aristocratic birth, had set himself to write novels which portrayed the cynicism and hardness of the upper classes in France. One of these novels, Sibylle, excited the anger of George Sand. She had not known Feuillet before; yet now she sought him out, at first in order to berate him for his book, but in the end to add him to her variegated string of lovers.

It has been said of Feuillet that he was a sort of "domesticated Musset." At any rate, he was far less sensitive than Musset, and George Sand was about seventeen years his senior. They parted after a short time, she going her way as a writer of novels that were very different from her earlier ones, while Feuillet grew more and more cynical and even stern, as he lashed the abnormal, neuropathic men and women about him.

The last great emotional crisis in George Sand's life was that which centers around her relations with Frederic Chopin. Chopin was the greatest genius who ever loved her. It is rather odd that he loved her. She had known him for two years, and had not seriously thought of him, though there is a story that when she first met him she kissed him before he had even been presented to her. She waited two years, and in those two years she had three lovers. Then at last she once more met Chopin, when he was in a state of melancholy, because a Polish girl had proved unfaithful to him.

It was the psychological moment; for this other woman, who was a devourer of hearts, found him at a piano, improvising a lamentation. George Sand stood beside him, listening. When he finished and looked up at her, their eyes met. She bent down without a word and kissed him on the lips.

What was she like when he saw her then? Grenier has described her in these words:

She was short and stout, but her face attracted all my attention, the eyes especially. They were wonderful eyes - a little too close together, it may be, large, with full eyelids, and black, very black, but by no means lustrous; they reminded me of unpolished marble, or rather of velvet, and this gave a strange, dull, even cold expression to her countenance. Her fine eyebrows and these great placid eyes gave her an air of strength and dignity which was not borne out by the lower part of her face. Her nose was rather thick and not over shapely. Her mouth was also rather coarse, and her chin small. She spoke with great simplicity, and her manners were very quiet.

Such as she was, she attached herself to Chopin for eight years. At first they traveled together very quietly to Majorca; and there, just as Musset had fallen ill at Venice, Chopin became feverish and an invalid. "Chopin coughs most gracefully," George Sand wrote of him, and again:

Chopin is the most inconstant of men. There is nothing

permanent about him but his cough.

It is not surprising if her nerves sometimes gave way. Acting as sick nurse, writing herself with rheumatic fingers, robbed by every one about her, and viewed with suspicion by the peasants because she did not go to church, she may be perhaps excused for her sharp words when, in fact, her deeds were kind.

Afterward, with Chopin, she returned to Paris, and the two lived openly together for seven years longer. An immense literature has grown around the subject of their relations. To this literature George Sand herself contributed very largely. Chopin never wrote a word; but what he failed to do, his friends and pupils did unsparingly.

Probably the truth is somewhat as one might expect. During the first period of fascination, George Sand was to Chopin what she had been to Sandeau and to Musset; and with her strange and subtle ways, she had undermined his health. But afterward that sort of love died out, and was succeeded by something like friendship. At any rate, this woman showed, as she had shown to others, a vast maternal kindness. She writes to him finally as "your old woman," and she does wonders in the way of nursing and care.

But in 1847 came a break between the two. Whatever the mystery of it may be, it turns upon what Chopin said of Sand:

"I have never cursed any one, but now I am so weary of life that I am near cursing her. Yet she suffers, too, and more, because she grows older as she grows more wicked."

In 1848, Chopin gave his last concert in Paris, and in 1849 he died. According to some, he was the victim of a Messalina. According to others, it was only "Messalina" that had kept him alive so long.

However, with his death came a change in the nature of George Sand. Emotionally, she was an extinct volcano. Intellectually, she was at her very best. She no longer tore passions into tatters, but wrote naturally, simply, stories of country life and tales for children. In one of her books she has given an enduring picture of the Franco-Prussian War. There are many rather pleasant descriptions of her then, living at Nohant, where she made a curious figure, bustling about in ill-fitting costumes, and smoking interminable cigarettes.

She had lived much, and she had drunk deep of life, when she died in 1876. One might believe her to have been only a woman of perpetual liaisons. Externally she was this, and yet what did Balzac, that great master of human psychology, write of her in the intimacy of a private correspondence?

She is a female bachelor. She is an artist. She is generous. She is devoted. She is chaste. Her dominant characteristics are those of a man, and therefore, she is not to be regarded as a woman. She is an excellent mother, adored by her children. Morally, she is like a lad of twenty; for in her heart of hearts, she is more than chaste - she is a prude. It is only in externals that she comports herself as a Bohemian. All her follies are titles to glory in the eyes of those whose souls are noble.

A curious verdict this! Her love-life seems almost that of neither man nor woman, but of an animal. Yet whether she was in reality responsible for what she did, when we consider her strange heredity, her wretched marriage, the disillusions of her early life - who shall sit in judgment on her, since who knows all?

THE MYSTERY OF CHARLES DICKENS

Perhaps no public man in the English-speaking world, in the last century, was so widely and intimately known as Charles Dickens. From his eighteenth year, when he won his first success in journalism, down through his series of brilliant triumphs in fiction, he was more and more a conspicuous figure, living in the blaze of an intense publicity. He met every one and knew every one, and was the companion of every kind of man and woman. He loved to frequent the "caves of harmony" which Thackeray has immortalized, and he was a member of all the best Bohemian clubs of London. Actors, authors, good fellows generally, were his intimate friends, and his acquaintance extended far beyond into the homes of merchants and lawyers and the mansions of the proudest nobles. Indeed, he seemed to be almost a universal friend.

One remembers, for instance, how he was called in to arbitrate between Thackeray and George Augustus Sala, who had quarreled. One remembers how Lord Byron's daughter, Lady Lovelace, when upon her sick-bed, used to send for Dickens because there was something in his genial, sympathetic manner that soothed her. Crushing pieces of ice between her teeth in agony, she would speak to him and he would answer her in his rich, manly tones until she was comforted and felt able to endure more hours of pain without complaint.

Lyndon Orr

Dickens was a jovial soul. His books fairly steam with Christmas cheer and hot punch and the savor of plum puddings, very much as do his letters to his intimate friends. Everybody knew Dickens. He could not dine in public without attracting attention. When he left the dining-room, his admirers would descend upon his table and carry off egg-shells, orange-peels, and other things that remained behind, so that they might have memorials of this much-loved writer. Those who knew him only by sight would often stop him in the streets and ask the privilege of shaking hands with him; so different was he from - let us say - Tennyson, who was as great an Englishman in his way as Dickens, but who kept himself aloof and saw few strangers.

It is hard to associate anything like mystery with Dickens, though he was fond of mystery as an intellectual diversion, and his last unfinished novel was The Mystery of Edwin Drood. Moreover, no one admired more than he those complex plots which Wilkie Collins used to weave under the influence of laudanum. But as for his own life, it seemed so normal, so free from anything approaching mystery, that we can scarcely believe it to have been tinged with darker colors than those which appeared upon the surface.

A part of this mystery is plain enough. The other part is still obscure - or of such a character that one does not care to bring it wholly to the light. It had to do with his various relations with women.

The world at large thinks that it knows this chapter in the life of Dickens, and that it refers wholly to his unfortunate disagreement with his wife. To be sure, this is a chapter that is writ large in all of his biographies, and yet it is nowhere correctly told. His chosen biographer was John Forster, whose Life of Charles Dickens, in three volumes, must remain a standard work; but even Forster - we may assume through tact - has not set down all that he could, although he gives a clue.

As is well known, Dickens married Miss Catherine Hogarth when he was only twenty-four. He had just published his Sketches by Boz, the copyright of which he sold for one hundred pounds, and was beginning the Pickwick Papers. About this time his publisher brought N. P. Willis down to Furnival's Inn to see the man whom Willis called "a young paragraphist for the Morning Chronicle." Willis thus sketches Dickens and his surroundings:

In the most crowded part of Holborn, within a door or two of the Bull and Mouth Inn, we pulled up at the entrance of a large building used for lawyers' chambers. I followed by a long flight of stairs to an upper story, and was ushered into an uncarpeted and bleak-looking room, with a deal table, two or three chairs and a few books, a small boy and Mr. Dickens for the contents.

I was only struck at first with one thing - and I made a memorandum of it that evening as the strongest instance I had seen of English obsequiousness to employers - the degree to which the poor author was overpowered with the honor of his publisher's visit! I remember saying to myself, as I sat down on a rickety chair:

"My good fellow, if you were in America with that fine face and your ready quill, you would have no need to be condescended to by a publisher."

Dickens was dressed very much as he has since described Dick Swiveller, minus the swell look. His hair was cropped close to his head, his clothes scant, though jauntily cut, and, after changing a ragged office-coat for a shabby blue, he stood by the door, collarless and buttoned up, the very personification of a close sailer to the wind.

Before this interview with Willis, which Dickens always repudiated, he had become something of a celebrity among the newspaper men with whom he worked as a stenographer. As every one knows, he had had a hard time in his early years, working in a blacking-shop, and feeling too keenly the ignominious position of which a less sensitive boy would probably have thought nothing. Then he became a shorthand reporter, and was busy at his work, so that he had little time for amusements.

It has been generally supposed that no love-affair entered his life until he met Catherine Hogarth, whom he married soon after making her acquaintance. People who are eager at ferreting out unimportant facts about important men had unanimously come to the conclusion that up to the age of twenty Dickens was entirely fancy-free. It was left to an American to disclose the fact that this was not the case, but that even in his teens he had been captivated by a girl of about his own age.

Inasmuch as the only reproach that was ever made against Dickens was based upon his love-affairs, let us go back and trace them from this early one to the very last, which must yet for some years, at least, remain a mystery.

Everything that is known about his first affair is contained in a book very beautifully printed, but inaccessible to most readers. Some years ago Mr. William K. Bixby, of St. Louis, found in London a collector of curios. This man had in his stock a number of letters which had passed between a Miss Maria Beadnell and Charles Dickens when the two were about nineteen and a second package of letters representing a later acquaintance, about 1855, at which time Miss Beadnell had been married for a long time to a Mr. Henry Louis Winter, of 12 Artillery Place, London.

The copyright laws of Great Britain would not allow Mr. Bixby to publish the letters in that country, and he did not care to give them to the public here. Therefore, he presented them to the Bibliophile Society, with the understanding that four hundred and ninety-three copies, with the Bibliophile book-plate, were to be printed and distributed among the members of the society. A few additional copies were struck off, but these did not bear the Bibliophile book-plate. Only two copies are available for other readers, and to peruse these it is necessary to visit the Congressional Library in Washington, where they were placed on July 24, 1908.

These letters form two series - the first written to Miss Beadnell in or about 1829, and the second written to Mrs. Winter, formerly Miss Beadnell, in 1855.

The book also contains an introduction by Henry H. Harper, who sets forth some theories which the facts, in my opinion, do not support; and there are a number of interesting portraits, especially one of Miss Beadnell in 1829 - a lovely girl with dark curls. Another shows her in 1855, when she writes of herself as "old and fat" - thereby doing herself a great deal of injustice; for although she had lost her youthful beauty, she was a very presentable woman of middle age, but one who would not be particularly noticed in any company.

Summing up briefly these different letters, it may be said that in the first set Dickens wrote to the lady ardently, but by no means passionately. From what he says it is plain enough that she did not respond to his feeling, and that presently she left London and went to Paris, for her family was well-to-do, while Dickens was living from hand to mouth.

In the second set of letters, written long afterward, Mrs. Winter seems to have "set her cap" at the now famous author; but at that time he was courted by every one, and had long ago forgotten the lady who had so easily dismissed him in his younger days. In 1855, Mrs. Winter seems to have reproached him for not having been more constant in the past; but he replied:

You answered me coldly and reproachfully, and so I went my way.

Mr. Harper, in his introduction, tries very hard to prove that in writing David Copperfield Dickens drew the character of Dora from Miss Beadnell. It is a dangerous thing to say from whom any character in a novel is drawn. An author takes whatever suits his purpose in circumstance and fancy, and blends them all into one consistent whole, which is not to be identified with any individual. There is little reason to think that the most intimate friends of Dickens and of his family were mistaken through all the years when they were certain that the boy husband and the girl wife of David Copperfield were suggested by any one save Dickens himself and Catherine Hogarth.

Why should he have gone back to a mere passing fancy, to a girl who did not care for him, and who had no influence on his life, instead of picturing, as David's first wife, one whom he deeply loved, whom he married, who was the mother of his children, and who made a great part of his career, even that part which was inwardly half tragic and wholly mournful?

Miss Beadnell may have been the original of Flora in Little Dorrit, though even this is doubtful. The character was at the time ascribed to a Miss Anna Maria Leigh, whom Dickens sometimes flirted with and sometimes caricatured.

When Dickens came to know George Hogarth, who was one of his colleagues on the staff of the Morning Chronicle, he met Hogarth's daughters - Catherine, Georgina, and Mary - and at once fell ardently in love with Catherine, the eldest and prettiest of the three. He himself was almost girlish, with his fair complexion and light, wavy hair, so that the famous sketch by Maclise has a remarkable charm; yet nobody could really say with truth that any one of the three girls was beautiful. Georgina Hogarth, however, was sweet-tempered and of a motherly disposition. It may be that in a fashion she loved Dickens all her life, as she remained with him after he parted from her sister, taking the utmost care of his children, and looking out with unselfish fidelity for his many needs.

It was Mary, however, the youngest of the Hogarths, who lived with the Dickenses during the first twelvemonth of their married life. To Dickens she was like a favorite sister, and when she died very suddenly, in her eighteenth year, her loss was a great shock to him.

It was believed for a long time - in fact, until their separation - that Dickens and his wife were extremely happy in their home life. His writings glorified all that was domestic, and paid many tender tributes to the joys of family affection. When the separation came the whole world was shocked. And yet rather early in Dickens's married life there was more or less infelicity. In his Retrospections of an Active Life, Mr. John Bigelow writes a few sentences which are interesting for their frankness, and which give us certain hints:

Mrs. Dickens was not a handsome woman, though stout, hearty, and matronly; there was something a little doubtful about her eye, and I thought her endowed with a temper that might be very violent when roused, though not easily rousable. Mrs. Caulfield told me that a Miss Teman - I think that is the name - was the source of the difficulty between Mrs. Dickens and her husband. She played in private theatricals with Dickens, and he sent her a portrait in a brooch, which met with an accident requiring it to be sent to the jeweler's to be mended. The jeweler, noticing Mr. Dickens's initials, sent it to his house. Mrs. Dickens's sister, who had always been in love with him and was jealous of Miss Teman, told Mrs. Dickens of the brooch, and she mounted her husband with comb and brush. This, no doubt, was Mrs. Dickens's version, in the main.

A few evenings later I saw Miss Teman at the Haymarket Theatre, playing with Buckstone and Mr.

and Mrs. Charles Mathews. She seemed rather a small cause for such a serious result - passably pretty, and not much of an actress.

Here in one passage we have an intimation that Mrs. Dickens had a temper that was easily roused, that Dickens himself was interested in an actress, and that Miss Hogarth "had always been in love with him, and was jealous of Miss Teman."

Some years before this time, however, there had been growing in the mind of Dickens a certain formless discontent - something to which he could not give a name, yet which, cast over him the shadow of disappointment. He expressed the same feeling in David Copperfield, when he spoke of David's life with Dora. It seemed to come from the fact that he had grown to be a man, while his wife had still remained a child.

A passage or two may be quoted from the novel, so that we may set them beside passages in Dickens's own life, which we know to have referred to his own wife, and not to any such nebulous person as Mrs. Winter.

The shadow I have mentioned that was not to be between us any more, but was to rest wholly on my heart - how did that fall? The old unhappy feeling pervaded my life. It was deepened, if it were changed at all; but it was as undefined as ever, and addressed me like a strain of sorrowful music faintly heard in the night. I loved my wife dearly; but the happiness I had vaguely anticipated, once, was not the happiness I enjoyed, AND THERE WAS ALWAYS SOMETHING WANTING.

What I missed I still regarded as something that had

been a dream of my youthful fancy; that was incapable of realization; that I was now discovering to be so, with some natural pain, as all men did. But that it would have been better for me if my wife could have helped me more, and shared the many thoughts in which I had no partner, and that this might have been I knew.

What I am describing slumbered and half awoke and slept again in the innermost recesses of my mind. There was no evidence of it to me; I knew of no influence it had in anything I said or did. I bore the weight of all our little cares and all my projects.

"There can be no disparity in marriage like unsuitability of mind and purpose." These words I remembered. I had endeavored to adapt Dora to myself, and found it impracticable. It remained for me to adapt myself to Dora; to share with her what I could, and be happy; to bear on my own shoulders what I must, and be still happy.

Thus wrote Dickens in his fictitious character, and of his fictitious wife. Let us see how he wrote and how he acted in his own person, and of his real wife.

As early as 1856, he showed a curious and restless activity, as of one who was trying to rid himself of unpleasant thoughts. Mr. Forster says that he began to feel a strain upon his invention, a certain disquietude, and a necessity for jotting down memoranda in note-books, so as to assist his memory and his imagination. He began to long for solitude. He would take long, aimless rambles into the country, returning at no particular time or season. He once wrote to Forster:

I have had dreadful thoughts of getting away some-where altogether by myself. If I could have managed it, I think I might have gone to the Pyrenees for six months. I have visions of living for half a year or so in all sorts of inaccessible places, and of opening a new book therein. A floating idea of going up above the snow-line, and living in some astonishing convent, hovers over me.

What do these cryptic utterances mean? At first, both in his novel and in his letters, they are obscure; but before long, in each, they become very definite. In 1856, we find these sentences among his letters:

The old days - the old days! Shall I ever, I wonder, get the frame of mind back as it used to be then? Something of it, perhaps, but never quite as it used to be.

I find that the skeleton in my domestic closet is becoming a pretty big one.

His next letter draws the veil and shows plainly what he means:

Poor Catherine and I are not made for each other, and there is no help for it. It is not only that she makes me uneasy and unhappy, but that I make her so, too - and much more so. We are strangely ill-assorted for the bond that exists between us.

Then he goes on to say that she would have been a thousand times happier if she had been married to another man. He speaks of "incompatibility," and a "difference of temperaments." In fact, it is the same old story with which we have become so familiar, and which is both as old as the hills and as new as this morning's newspaper.

Naturally, also, things grow worse, rather than better. Dickens comes to speak half jocularly of "the plunge," and calculates as to what effect it will have on his public readings. He kept back the announcement of "the plunge" until after he had given several readings; then, on April 29, 1858, Mrs. Dickens left his home. His eldest son went to live with the mother, but the rest of the children remained with their father, while his daughter Mary nominally presided over the house. In the background, however, Georgina Hogarth, who seemed all through her life to have cared for Dickens more than for her sister, remained as a sort of guide and guardian for his children.

This arrangement was a private matter, and should not have been brought to public attention; but it was impossible to suppress all gossip about so prominent a man. Much of the gossip was exaggerated; and when it came to the notice of Dickens it stung him so severely as to lead him into issuing a public justification of his course. He published a statement in Household Words, which led to many other letters in other periodicals, and finally a long one from him, which was printed in the New York Tribune, addressed to his friend Mr. Arthur Smith.

Dickens afterward declared that he had written this letter as a strictly personal and private one, in order to correct false rumors and scandals. Mr. Smith naturally thought that the statement was intended for publication, but Dickens always spoke of it as "the violated letter."

By his allusions to a difference of temperament and to incompatibility, Dickens no doubt meant that his wife had ceased to be to him the same companion that she had been in days gone by. As in so many cases, she had not changed, while he had. He had grown out of the sphere in which he had been born, "associated with blacking-boys and quilt-printers," and had become one of the great men of his time, whose genius was universally admired.

Mr. Bigelow saw Mrs. Dickens as she really was - a commonplace woman endowed with the temper of a vixen, and disposed to outbursts of actual violence when her jealousy was roused.

It was impossible that the two could have remained together, when in intellect and sympathy they were so far apart. There is nothing strange about their separation, except the exceedingly bad taste with which Dickens made it a public affair. It is safe to assume that he felt the need of a different mate; and that he found one is evident enough from the hints and bits of innuendo that are found in the writings of his contemporaries.

He became a pleasure-lover; but more than that, he needed one who could understand his moods and match them, one who could please his tastes, and one who could give him that admiration which he felt to be his due; for he was always anxious to be praised, and his letters are full of anecdotes relating to his love of praise.

One does not wish to follow out these clues too closely. It is certain that neither Miss Beadnell as a girl nor Mrs. Winter as a matron made any serious appeal to him. The actresses who have been often mentioned in connection with his name were, for the most part, mere passing favorites. The woman who in life was Dora made him feel the same incompleteness that he has described in his best-known book. The companion to whom he clung in his later years was neither a light-minded creature like Miss Beadnell, nor an undeveloped, high-tempered woman like the one he married, nor a mere domestic, friendly creature like Georgina Hogarth.

Ought we to venture upon a quest which shall solve this mystery in the life of Charles Dickens! In his last will and testament, drawn up and signed by him about a year before his death, the first paragraph reads as follows:

I, Charles Dickens, of Gadshill Place, Higham, in the county of Kent, hereby revoke all my former wills and codicils and declare this to be my last will and testament. I give the sum of one thousand pounds, free of legacy duty, to Miss Ellen Lawless Ternan, late of Houghton Place, Ampthill Square, in the county of Middlesex.

In connection with this, read Mr. John Bigelow's careless jottings made some fifteen years before. Remember the Miss "Teman," about whose name he was not quite certain; the Hogarth sisters' dislike of her; and the mysterious figure in the background of the novelist's later life. Then consider the first bequest in his will, which leaves a substantial sum to one who was neither a relative nor a subordinate, but - may we assume - more than an ordinary friend?

HONORE DE BALZAC AND EVELINA HANSKA

I remember once, when editing an elaborate work on literature, that the publisher called me into his private office. After the door was closed, he spoke in tones of suppressed emotion.

"Why is it," said he, "that you have such a lack of proportion? In the selection you have made I find that only two pages are given to George P. Morris, while you haven't given E. P. Roe any space at all! Yet, look here - you've blocked out fifty pages for Balzac, who was nothing but an immoral Frenchman!"

I adjusted this difficulty, somehow or other - I do not just remember how - and began to think that, after all, this publisher's view of things was probably that of the English and American public. It is strange that so many biographies and so many appreciations of the greatest novelist who ever lived should still have left him, in the eyes of the reading public, little more than "an immoral Frenchman."

"In Balzac," said Taine, "there was a money-broker, an archeologist, an architect, an upholsterer, a tailor, an old-clothes dealer, a journeyman apprentice, a physician, and a notary." Balzac was also a mystic, a supernaturalist, and, above all, a consummate artist. No one who is all these things in high measure, and who has raised himself by his genius above his countrymen, deserves the censure of my former publisher.

Still less is Balzac to be dismissed as "immoral," for his life was one of singular self-sacrifice in spite of much temptation. His face was strongly sensual, his look and bearing denoted almost savage power; he led a free life in a country which allowed much freedom; and yet his story is almost mystic in its fineness of thought, and in its detachment, which was often that of another world.

Balzac was born in 1799, at Tours, with all the traits of the people of his native province - fond of eating and drinking, and with plenty of humor. His father was fairly well off. Of four children, our Balzac was the eldest. The third was his sister Laure, who throughout his life was the most intimate friend he had, and to whom we owe his rescue from much scandalous and untrue gossip. From her we learn that their father was a combination of Montaigne, Rabelais, and "Uncle Toby."

Young Balzac went to a clerical school at seven, and stayed there for seven years. Then he was brought home, apparently much prostrated, although the good fathers could find nothing physically amiss with him, and nothing in his studies to account for his agitation. No one ever did discover just what was the matter, for he seemed well enough in the next few years, basking on the riverside, watching the activities of his native town, and thoroughly studying the rustic types that he was afterward to make familiar to the world. In fact, in Louis Lambert he has set before us a picture of his own boyish life, very much as Dickens did of his in David Copperfield.

For some reason, when these years were over, the boy began to have what is so often known as "a call" - a sort of instinct that he was to attain renown. Unfortunately it happened that about this time (1814) he and his parents removed to Paris, which was his home by choice, until his death in 1850. He studied here under famous teachers, and gave three years to the pursuit of law, of which he was very fond as literary material, though he refused to practise.

This was the more grievous, since a great part of the family property had been lost. The Balzacs were afflicted by actual poverty, and Honore endeavored, with his pen, to beat the wolf back from the door. He earned a little money with pamphlets and occasional stories, but his thirst for fame was far from satisfied. He was sure that he was called to literature, and yet he was not sure that he had the power to succeed. In one of his letters to his sister, he wrote:

I am young and hungry, and there is nothing on my plate. Oh, Laure, Laure, my two boundless desires, my only ones - to be famous, and to be loved - they ever be satisfied?

For the next ten years he was learning his trade, and the artistic use of the fiction writer's tools. What is more to the point, is the fact that he began to dream of a series of great novels, which should give a true and panoramic picture of the whole of human life. This was the first intimation of his "Human Comedy," which was so daringly undertaken and so nearly completed in his after years. In his early days of obscurity, he said to his readers:

Note well the characters that I introduce, since you will

have to follow their fortunes through thirty novels that are to come.

Here we see how little he had been daunted by ill success, and how his prodigious imagination had not been overcome by sorrow and evil fortune. Meantime, writing almost savagely, and with a feeling combined of ambition and despair, he had begun, very slowly indeed, to create a public. These ten years, however, had loaded him with debts; and his struggle to keep himself afloat only plunged him deeper in the mire. His thirty unsigned novels began to pay him a few hundred francs, not in cash, but in promissory notes; so that he had to go still deeper into debt.

In 1827 he was toiling on his first successful novel, and indeed one of the best historic novels in French literature - The Chouans. He speaks of his labor as "done with a tired brain and an anxious mind," and of the eight or ten business letters that he had to write each day before he could begin his literary work.

"Postage and an omnibus are extravagances that I cannot allow myself," he writes. "I stay at home so as not to wear out my clothes. Is that clear to you?"

At the end of the next year, though he was already popular as a novelist, and much sought out by people of distinction, he was at the very climax of his poverty. He had written thirty-five books, and was in debt to the amount of a hundred and twenty-four thousand francs. He was saved from bankruptcy only by the aid of Mme. de Berny, a woman of high character, and one whose moral influence was very strong with Balzac until her early death.

The relation between these two has a sweetness and a purity which are seldom found. Mme. de Berny gave Balzac money as she would have given it to a son, and thereby she saved a great soul for literature. But there was no sickly sentiment between them, and Balzac regarded her with a noble love which he has expressed in the character of Mme. Firmiani.

It was immediately after she had lightened his burdens that the real Balzac comes before us in certain stories which have no equal, and which are among the most famous that he ever wrote. What could be more wonderful than his El Verdugo, which gives us a brief horror while compelling our admiration? What, outside of Balzac himself, could be more terrible than Gobseck, a frightful study of avarice, containing a deathbed scene which surpasses in dreadfulness almost anything in literature? Add to these A Passion in the Desert, The Girl with the Golden Eyes, The Droll Stories, The Red Inn, and The Magic Skin, and you have a cluster of masterpieces not to be surpassed.

In the year 1829, when he was just beginning to attain a slight success, Balzac received a long letter written in a woman's hand. As he read it, there came to him something very like an inspiration, so full of understanding were the written words, so full of appreciation and of sympathy with the best that he had done. This anonymous note pointed out here and there such defects as are apt to become chronic with a young author. Balzac was greatly stirred by its keen and sympathetic criticism. No one before had read his soul so clearly. No one - not even his devoted sister, Laure de Surville - had judged his work so wisely, had come so closely to his deepest feeling.

He read the letter over and over, and presently another came, full of critical appreciation, and of wholesome, tonic, frank, friendly words of cheer. It was very largely the effect of these letters that roused Balzac's full powers and made him sure of winning the two great objects of his first ambition - love and fame - the ideals of the chivalrous, romantic Frenchman from Caesar's time down to the present day.

Other letters followed, and after a while their authorship was made known to Balzac. He learned that they had been written by a young Polish lady, Mme. Evelina Hanska, the wife of a Polish count, whose health was feeble, and who spent much time in Switzerland because the climate there agreed with him.

He met her first at Neuchatel, and found her all that he had imagined. It is said that she had no sooner raised her face, and looked him fully in the eyes, than she fell fainting to the floor, overcome by her emotion. Balzac himself was deeply moved. From that day until their final meeting he wrote to her daily.

The woman who had become his second soul was not beautiful. Nevertheless, her face was intensely spiritual, and there was a mystic quality about it which made a strong appeal to Balzac's innermost nature. Those who saw him in Paris knocking about the streets at night with his boon companions, hobnobbing with the elder Dumas, or rejecting the frank advances of George Sand, would never have dreamed of this mysticism.

Balzac was heavy and broad of figure. His face was suggestive only of what was sensuous and sensual. At the same time, those few who looked into his heart and mind found there many a sign of the fine inner strain which purified the grosser elements of his nature. He who wrote the roaring Rabelaisian Contes Drolatiques was likewise the author of Seraphita.

This mysticism showed itself in many things that Balzac did. One little incident will perhaps be sufficiently characteristic of many others. He had a belief that names had a sort of esoteric appropriateness. So, in selecting them for his novels, he gathered them with infinite pains from many sources, and then weighed them anxiously in the balance. A writer on the subject of names and their significance has given the following account of this trait:

The great novelist once spent an entire day tramping about in the remotest quarters of Paris in search of a fitting name for a character just conceived by him. Every sign-board, every door-plate, every affiche upon the walls, was scrutinized. Thousands of names were considered and rejected, and it was only after his companion, utterly worn out by fatigue, had flatly refused to drag his weary limbs through more than one additional street, that Balzac suddenly saw upon a sign the name "Marcas," and gave a shout of joy at having finally secured what he was seeking.

Marcas it was, from that moment; and Balzac gradually evolved a Christian name for him. First he considered what initial was most appropriate; and then, having decided upon Z, he went on to expand this into Zepherin, explaining minutely just why the whole name Zepherin Marcas, was the only possible one for the character in the novel.

In many ways Balzac and Evelina Hanska were mated

by nature. Whether they were fully mated the facts of their lives must demonstrate. For the present, the novelist plunged into a whirl of literary labor, toiling as few ever toiled - constructing several novels at the same time, visiting all the haunts of the French capital, so that he might observe and understand every type of human being, and then hurling himself like a giant at his work.

He had a curious practise of reading proofs. These would come to him in enormous sheets, printed on special paper, and with wide margins for his corrections. An immense table stood in the midst of his study, and upon the top he would spread out the proofs as if they were vast maps. Then, removing most of his outer garments, he would lie, face down, upon the proof-sheets, with a gigantic pencil, such as Bismarck subsequently used to wield. Thus disposed, he would go over the proofs.

Hardly anything that he had written seemed to suit him when he saw it in print. He changed and kept changing, obliterating what he disliked, writing in new sentences, revising others, and adding whole pages in the margins, until perhaps he had practically made a new book. This process was repeated several times; and how expensive it was may be judged from the fact that his bill for "author's proof corrections" was sometimes more than the publishers had agreed to pay him for the completed volume.

Sometimes, again, he would begin writing in the afternoon, and continue until dawn. Then, weary, aching in every bone, and with throbbing head, he would rise and turn to fall upon his couch after his eighteen hours of steady toil. But the memory of

Evelina Hanska always came to him; and with half-numbed fingers he would seize his pen, and forget his weariness in the pleasure of writing to the dark-eyed woman who drew him to her like a magnet.

These are very curious letters that Balzac wrote to Mme. Hanska. He literally told her everything about himself. Not only were there long passages instinct with tenderness, and with his love for her; but he also gave her the most minute account of everything that occurred, and that might interest her. Thus he detailed at length his mode of living, the clothes he wore, the people whom he met, his trouble with his creditors, the accounts of his income and outgo. One might think that this was egotism on his part; but it was more than that. It was a strong belief that everything which concerned him must concern her; and he begged her in turn to write as freely and as fully.

Mme. Hanska was not the only woman who became his friend and comrade, and to whom he often wrote. He made many acquaintances in the fashionable world through the good offices of the Duchesse de Castries. By her favor, he studied with his microscopic gaze the beau monde of Louis Philippe's rather unimpressive court.

In a dozen books he scourged the court of the citizen king - its pretensions, its commonness, and its assemblage of nouveaux riches. Yet in it he found many friends - Victor Hugo, the Girardins - and among them women who were of the world. George Sand he knew very well, and she made ardent love to him; but he laughed her off very much as the elder Dumas did.

Then there was the pretty, dainty Mme. Carraud, who

Lyndon Orr

read and revised his manuscripts, and who perhaps took a more intimate interest in him than did the other ladies whom he came to know so well. Besides Mme. Hanska, he had another correspondent who signed herself "Louise," but who never let him know her name, though she wrote him many piquant, sunny letters, which he so sadly needed.

For though Honore de Balzac was now one of the most famous writers of his time, his home was still a den of suffering. His debts kept pressing on him, loading him down, and almost quenching hope. He acted toward his creditors like a man of honor, and his physical strength was still that of a giant. To Mme. Carraud he once wrote the half pathetic, half humorous plaint:

Poor pen! It must be diamond, not because one would wish to wear it, but because it has had so much use!

And again:

Here I am, owing a hundred thousand francs. And I am forty!

Balzac and Mme. Hanska met many times after that first eventful episode at Neuchatel. It was at this time that he gave utterance to the poignant cry:

Love for me is life, and to-day I feel it more than ever!

In like manner he wrote, on leaving her, that famous epigram:

It is only the last love of a woman that can satisfy the first love of a man.

In 1842 Mme. Hanska's husband died. Balzac naturally expected that an immediate marriage with the countess would take place; but the woman who had loved him mystically for twelve years, and with a touch of the physical for nine, suddenly draws back. She will not promise anything. She talks of delays, owing to the legal arrangements for her children. She seems almost a prude. An American critic has contrasted her attitude with his:

Every one knows how utterly and absolutely Balzac devoted to this one woman all his genius, his aspiration, the thought of his every moment; how every day, after he had labored like a slave for eighteen hours, he would take his pen and pour out to her the most intimate details of his daily life; how at her call he would leave everything and rush across the continent to Poland or to Italy, being radiantly happy if he could but see her face and be for a few days by her side. The very thought of meeting her thrilled him to the very depths of his nature, and made him, for weeks and even months beforehand, restless, uneasy, and agitated, with an almost painful happiness.

It is the most startling proof of his immense vitality, both physical and mental, that so tremendous an emotional strain could be endured by him for years without exhausting his fecundity or blighting his creativeness.

With Balzac, however, it was the period of his most brilliant work; and this was true in spite of the anguish of long separations, and the complaints excited by what appears to be caprice or boldness or a faint indifference. Even in Balzac one notices toward the last a certain sense of strain underlying what he wrote, a certain lack of elasticity and facility, if of nothing more; yet on the whole it is likely that without this friendship Balzac would have been less great than he actually became, as it is certain that had it been broken off he would have ceased to write or to care for anything whatever in the world.

And yet, when they were free to marry, Mme. Hanska shrank away. Not until 1846, four years after her husband's death, did she finally give her promise to the eager Balzac. Then, in the overflow of his happiness, his creative genius blazed up into a most wonderful flame; but he soon discovered that the promise was not to be at once fulfilled. The shock impaired that marvelous vitality which had carried him through debt, and want, and endless labor.

It was at this moment, by the irony of fate, that his country hailed him as one of the greatest of its men of genius. A golden stream poured into his lap. His debts were not all extinguished, but his income was so large that they burdened him no longer.

But his one long dream was the only thing for which he cared; and though in an exoteric sense this dream came true, its truth was but a mockery. Evelina Hanska summoned him to Poland, and Balzac went to her at once. There was another long delay, and for more than a year he lived as a guest in the countess's mansion at Wierzchownia; but finally, in March, 1850, the two were married. A few weeks later they came back to France together, and occupied the little country house, Les Jardies, in which, some decades later, occurred Gambetta's mysterious death.

What is the secret of this strange love, which in the

woman seems to be not precisely love, but something else? Balzac was always eager for her presence. She, on the other hand, seems to have been mentally more at ease when he was absent. Perhaps the explanation, if we may venture upon one, is based upon a well-known physiological fact.

Love in its completeness is made up of two great elements - first, the element that is wholly spiritual, that is capable of sympathy, and tenderness, and deep emotion. The other element is the physical, the source of passion, of creative energy, and of the truly virile qualities, whether it be in man or woman. Now, let either of these elements be lacking, and love itself cannot fully and utterly exist. The spiritual nature in one may find its mate in the spiritual nature of another; and the physical nature of one may find its mate in the physical nature of another. But into unions such as these, love does not enter in its completeness. If there is any element lacking in either of those who think that they can mate, their mating will be a sad and pitiful failure.

It is evident enough that Mme. Hanska was almost wholly spiritual, and her long years of waiting had made her understand the difference between Balzac and herself. Therefore, she shrank from his proximity, and from his physical contact, and it was perhaps better for them both that their union was so quickly broken off by death; for the great novelist died of heart disease only five months after the marriage.

If we wish to understand the mystery of Balzac's life - or, more truly, the mystery of the life of the woman whom he married - take up and read once more the pages of Seraphita, one of his poorest novels and yet a singularly illuminating story, shedding light upon a secret of the soul.

CHARLES READE AND LAURA SEYMOUR

The instances of distinguished men, or of notable women, who have broken through convention in order to find a fitting mate, are very numerous. A few of these instances may, perhaps, represent what is usually called a Platonic union. But the evidence is always doubtful. The world is not possessed of abundant charity, nor does human experience lead one to believe that intimate relations between a man and a woman are compatible with Platonic friendship.

Perhaps no case is more puzzling than that which is found in the life-history of Charles Reade and Laura Seymour.

Charles Reade belongs to that brilliant group of English writers and artists which included Dickens, Bulwer-Lytton, Wilkie Collins, Tom Taylor, George Eliot, Swinburne, Sir Walter Besant, Maclise, and Goldwin Smith. In my opinion, he ranks next to Dickens in originality and power. His books are little read to-day; yet he gave to the English stage the comedy "Masks and Faces," which is now as much a classic as Goldsmith's "She Stoops to Conquer" or Sheridan's "School for Scandal." His power as a novelist was marvelous. Who can forget the madhouse episodes in Hard Cash, or the great trial scene in Griffith Gaunt, or that wonderful picture, in The

Cloister and the Hearth, of Germany and Rome at the end of the Middle Ages? Here genius has touched the dead past and made it glow again with an intense reality.

He was the son of a country gentleman, the lord of a manor which had been held by his family before the Wars of the Boses. His ancestors had been noted for their services in warfare, in Parliament, and upon the bench. Reade, therefore, was in feeling very much of an aristocrat. Sometimes he pushed his ancestral pride to a whimsical excess, very much as did his own creation, Squire Raby, in Put Yourself in His Place.

At the same time he might very well have been called a Tory democrat. His grandfather had married the daughter of a village blacksmith, and Reade was quite as proud of this as he was of the fact that another ancestor had been lord chief justice of England. From the sturdy strain which came to him from the blacksmith he, perhaps, derived that sledge-hammer power with which he wrote many of his most famous chapters, and which he used in newspaper contro-versies with his critics. From his legal ancestors there may have come to him the love of litigation, which kept him often in hot water. From those who had figured in the life of royal courts, he inherited a romantic nature, a love of art, and a very delicate perception of the niceties of cultivated usage. Such was Charles Reade - keen observer, scholar, Bohemian - a man who could be both rough and tender, and whose boisterous ways never concealed his warm heart.

Reade's school-days were Spartan in their severity. A teacher with the appropriate name of Slatter set him hard tasks and caned him unmercifully for every shortcoming. A weaker nature would have been crushed. Reade's was toughened, and he learned to resist pain and to resent wrong, so that hatred of injustice has been called his dominating trait.

In preparing himself for college he was singularly fortunate in his tutors. One of them was Samuel Wilberforce, afterward Bishop of Oxford, nicknamed, from his suavity of manner, "Soapy Sam"; and afterward, when Reade was studying law, his instructor was Samuel Warren, the author of that once famous novel, Ten Thousand a Year, and the creator of "Tittlebat Titmouse."

For his college at Oxford, Reade selected one of the most beautiful and ancient - Magdalen - which he entered, securing what is known as a demyship. Reade won his demyship by an extraordinary accident. Always an original youth, his reading was varied and valuable; but in his studies he had never tried to be minutely accurate in small matters. At that time every candidate was supposed to be able to repeat, by heart, the "Thirty-Nine Articles." Reade had no taste for memorizing; and out of the whole thirty-nine he had learned but three. His general examination was good, though not brilliant. When he came to be questioned orally, the examiner, by a chance that would not occur once in a million times, asked the candidate to repeat these very articles. Reade rattled them off with the greatest glibness, and produced so favorable an impression that he was let go without any further questioning.

It must be added that his English essay was original, and this also helped him; but had it not been for the other great piece of luck he would, in Oxford phrase, have been "completely gulfed." As it was, however, he was placed as highly as the young men who were afterward known as Cardinal Newman and Sir Robert Lowe (Lord Sherbrooke).

At the age of twenty-one, Reade obtained a fellowship, which entitled him to an income so long as he remained unmarried. It is necessary to consider the significance of this when we look at his subsequent career. The fellowship at Magdalen was worth, at the outset, about twelve hundred dollars annually, and it gave him possession of a suite of rooms free of any charge. He likewise secured a Vinerian fellowship in law, to which was attached an income of four hundred dollars. As time went on, the value of the first fellowship increased until it was worth twenty-five hundred dollars. Therefore, as with many Oxford men of his time, Charles Reade, who had no other fortune, was placed in this position - if he refrained from marrying, he had a home and a moderate income for life, without any duties whatsoever. If he married, he must give up his income and his comfortable apartments, and go out into the world and struggle for existence.

There was the further temptation that the possession of his fellowship did not even necessitate his living at Oxford. He might spend his time in London, or even outside of England, knowing that his chambers at Magdalen were kept in order for him, as a resting-place to which he might return whenever he chose.

Reade remained a while at Oxford, studying books and men - especially the latter. He was a great favorite with the undergraduates, though less so with the dons. He loved the boat-races on the river; he was a prodigious cricket-player, and one of the best bowlers of his time. He utterly refused to put on any of the academic dignity which his associates affected. He wore loud clothes. His flaring scarfs were viewed as being almost scandalous, very much as Longfellow's parti-colored waistcoats were regarded when he first came to Harvard as a professor.

Charles Reade pushed originality to eccentricity. He had a passion for violins, and ran himself into debt because he bought so many and such good ones. Once, when visiting his father's house at Ipsden, he shocked the punctilious old gentleman by dancing on the dining-table to the accompaniment of a fiddle, which he scraped delightedly. Dancing, indeed, was another of his diversions, and, in spite of the fact that he was a fellow of Magdalen and a D.C.L. of Oxford, he was always ready to caper and to display the new steps.

In the course of time, he went up to London; and at once plunged into the seething tide of the metropolis. He made friends far and wide, and in every class and station - among authors and politicians, bishops and bargees, artists and musicians. Charles Reade learned much from all of them, and all of them were fond of him.

But it was the theater that interested him most. Nothing else seemed to him quite so fine as to be a successful writer for the stage. He viewed the drama with all the reverence of an ancient Greek. On his tombstone he caused himself to be described as "Dramatist, novelist, journalist."

"Dramatist" he put first of all, even after long experience had shown him that his greatest power lay in writing novels. But in this early period he still hoped for fame upon the stage.

It was not a fortunate moment for dramatic writers. Plays were bought outright by the managers, who were afraid to risk any considerable sum, and were very shy about risking anything at all. The system had not yet been established according to which an author receives a share of the money taken at the box-office. Consequently, Reade had little or no financial success. He adapted several pieces from the French, for which he was paid a few bank-notes. "Masks and Faces" got a hearing, and drew large audiences, but Reade had sold it for a paltry sum; and he shared the honors of its authorship with Tom Taylor, who was then much better known.

Such was the situation. Reade was personally liked, but his plays were almost all rejected. He lived somewhat extravagantly and ran into debt, though not very deeply. He had a play entitled "Christie Johnstone," which he believed to be a great one, though no manager would venture to produce it. Reade, brooding, grew thin and melancholy. Finally, he decided that he would go to a leading actress at one of the principal theaters and try to interest her in his rejected play. The actress he had in mind was Laura Seymour, then appearing at the Haymarket under the management of Buckstone; and this visit proved to be the turning-point in Reade's whole life.

Laura Seymour was the daughter of a surgeon at Bath - a man in large practise and with a good income, every penny of which he spent. His family lived in lavish style; but one morning, after he had sat up all night playing cards, his little daughter found him in the dining-room, stone dead. After his funeral it appeared that he had left no provision for his family. A friend of his - a Jewish gentleman of Portuguese extraction - showed much kindness to the children, settling their affairs and leaving them with some money in the bank; but, of course, something must be done.

The two daughters removed to London, and at a very early age Laura had made for herself a place in the dramatic world, taking small parts at first, but rising so rapidly that in her fifteenth year she was cast for the part of Juliet. As an actress she led a life of strange vicissitudes. At one time she would be pinched by poverty, and at another time she would be well supplied with money, which slipped through her fingers like water. She was a true Bohemian, a happy-go-lucky type of the actors of her time.

From all accounts, she was never very beautiful; but she had an instinct for strange, yet effective, costumes, which attracted much attention. She has been described as "a fluttering, buoyant, gorgeous little butterfly." Many were drawn to her. She was careless of what she did, and her name was not untouched with scandal. But she lived through it all, and emerged a clever, sympathetic woman of wide experience, both on the stage and off it.

One of her admirers - an elderly gentleman named Seymour - came to her one day when she was in much need of money, and told her that he had just deposited a thousand pounds to her credit at the bank. Having said this, he left the room precipitately. It was the beginning of a sort of courtship; and after a while she married him. Her feeling toward him was one of gratitude. There was no sentiment about it; but she made him a good wife, and gave no further cause for gossip.

Such was the woman whom Charles Reade now approached with the request that she would let him read to her a portion of his play. He had seen her act, and he honestly believed her to be a dramatic genius of the first order. Few others shared this belief; but she was generally thought of as a competent, though by no means brilliant, actress. Reade admired her extremely, so that at the very thought of speaking with her his emotions almost choked him.

In answer to a note, she sent word that he might call at her house. He was at this time (1849) in his thirty-eighth year. The lady was a little older, and had lost something of her youthful charm; yet, when Reade was ushered into her drawing-room, she seemed to him the most graceful and accomplished woman whom he had ever met.

She took his measure, or she thought she took it, at a glance. Here was one of those would-be playwrights who live only to torment managers and actresses. His face was thin, from which she inferred that he was probably half starved. His bashfulness led her to suppose that he was an inexperienced youth. Little did she imagine that he was the son of a landed proprietor, a fellow of one of Oxford's noblest colleges, and one with friends far higher in the world than herself. Though she thought so little of him, and quite expected to be bored, she settled herself in a soft armchair to listen. The unsuccessful playwright read to her a scene or two from his still unfinished drama. She heard him patiently, noting the cultivated accent of his voice, which proved to her that he was at least a gentleman.

When he had finished, she said:

"Yes, that's good! The plot is excellent." Then she laughed a sort of stage laugh, and remarked lightly: "Why don't you turn it into a novel?"

Reade was stung to the quick. Nothing that she could have said would have hurt him more. Novels he despised; and here was this woman, the queen of the English stage, as he regarded her, laughing at his drama and telling him to make a novel of it. He rose and bowed.

"I am trespassing on your time," he said; and, after barely touching the fingers of her outstretched hand, he left the room abruptly.

The woman knew men very well, though she scarcely knew Charles Reade. Something in his melancholy and something in his manner stirred her heart. It was not a heart that responded to emotions readily, but it was a very good-natured heart. Her explanation of Reade's appearance led her to think that he was very poor. If she had not much tact, she had an abundant store of sympathy; and so she sat down and wrote a very blundering but kindly letter, in which she enclosed a five-pound note.

Reade subsequently described his feelings on receiving this letter with its bank-note. He said:

"I, who had been vice-president of Magdalen - I, who flattered myself I was coming to the fore as a dramatist - to have a five-pound note flung at my head, like a ticket for soup to a pauper, or a bone to a dog, and by an actress, too! Yet she said my reading was admirable; and, after all, there is much virtue in a five-pound note. Anyhow, it showed the writer had a good heart."

The more he thought of her and of the incident, the more comforted he was. He called on her the next day without making an appointment; and when she received him, he had the five-pound note fluttering in his hand.

She started to speak, but he interrupted her.

"No," he said, "that is not what I wanted from you. I wanted sympathy, and you have unintentionally supplied it."

Then this man, whom she had regarded as half starved, presented her with an enormous bunch of hothouse grapes, and the two sat down and ate them together, thus beginning a friendship which ended only with Laura Seymour's death.

Oddly enough, Mrs. Seymour's suggestion that Reade should make a story of his play was a suggestion which he actually followed. It was to her guidance and sympathy that the world owes the great novels which he afterward composed. If he succeeded on the stage at all, it was not merely in "Masks and Faces," but in his powerful dramatization of Zola's novel, L'Assommoir, under the title "Drink," in which the late Charles Warner thrilled and horrified great audiences all over the English-speaking world. Had Reade never known Laura Seymour, he might never have written so strong a drama.

The mystery of Reade's relations with this woman can

never be definitely cleared up. Her husband, Mr. Seymour, died not long after she and Reade became acquainted. Then Reade and several friends, both men and women, took a house together; and Laura Seymour, now a clever manager and amiable hostess, looked after all the practical affairs of the establishment. One by one, the others fell away, through death or by removal, until at last these two were left alone. Then Reade, unable to give up the companionship which meant so much to him, vowed that she must still remain and care for him. He leased a house in Sloane Street, which he has himself described in his novel A Terrible Temptation. It is the chapter wherein Reade also draws his own portrait in the character of Francis Bolfe:

The room was rather long, low, and nondescript; scarlet flock paper; curtains and sofas, green Utrecht velvet; woodwork and pillars, white and gold; two windows looking on the street; at the other end folding-doors, with scarcely any woodwork, all plate glass, but partly hidden by heavy curtains of the same color and material as the others.

At last a bell rang; the maid came in and invited Lady Bassett to follow her. She opened the glass folding-doors and took them into a small conservatory, walled like a grotto, with ferns sprouting out of rocky fissures, and spars sparkling, water dripping. Then she opened two more glass folding-doors, and ushered them into an empty room, the like of which Lady Bassett had never seen; it was large in itself, and multiplied tenfold by great mirrors from floor to ceiling, with no frames but a narrow oak beading; opposite her, on entering, was a bay window, all plate glass, the central panes of which opened, like doors, upon a pretty little garden that glowed with color, and was backed by fine trees belonging to the nation; for this garden ran up to the wall of Hyde Park.

The numerous and large mirrors all down to the ground laid hold of the garden and the flowers, and by double and treble reflection filled the room with delightful nooks of verdure and color.

Here are the words in which Reade describes himself as he looked when between fifty and sixty years of age:

He looked neither like a poet nor a drudge, but a great fat country farmer. He was rather tall, very portly, smallish head, commonplace features, mild brown eye not very bright, short beard, and wore a suit of tweed all one color.

Such was the house and such was the man over both of which Laura Seymour held sway until her death in 1879. What must be thought of their relations? She herself once said to Mr. John Coleman:

"As for our positions - his and mine - we are partners, nothing more. He has his bank-account, and I have mine. He is master of his fellowship and his rooms at Oxford, and I am mistress of this house, but not his mistress! Oh, dear, no!"

At another time, long after Mr. Seymour's death, she said to an intimate friend:

"I hope Mr. Reade will never ask me to marry him, for I should certainly refuse the offer."

There was no reason why he should not have made this offer, because his Oxford fellowship ceased to be important to him after he had won fame as a novelist. Publishers paid him large sums for everything he wrote. His debts were all paid off, and his income was assured. Yet he never spoke of marriage, and he always introduced his friend as "the lady who keeps my house for me."

As such, he invited his friends to meet her, and as such, she even accompanied him to Oxford. There was no concealment, and apparently there was nothing to conceal. Their manner toward each other was that of congenial friends. Mrs. Seymour, in fact, might well have been described as "a good fellow." Sometimes she referred to him as "the doctor," and sometimes by the nickname "Charlie." He, on his side, often spoke of her by her last name as "Seymour," precisely as if she had been a man. One of his relatives rather acutely remarked about her that she was not a woman of sentiment at all, but had a genius for friendship; and that she probably could not have really loved any man at all.

This is, perhaps, the explanation of their intimacy. If so, it is a very remarkable instance of Platonic friendship. It is certain that, after she met Reade, Mrs. Seymour never cared for any other man. It is no less certain that he never cared for any other woman. When she died, five years before his death, his life became a burden to him. It was then that he used to speak of her as "my lost darling" and "my dove." He directed that they should be buried side by side in Willesden churchyard. Over the monument which commemorates them both, he caused to be inscribed, in addition to an epitaph for himself, the following tribute to his friend.

One should read it and accept the touching words as answering every question that may be asked:

Here lies the great heart of Laura Seymour, a brilliant artist, a humble Christian, a charitable woman, a loving daughter, sister, and friend, who lived for others from her childhood. Tenderly pitiful to all God's creatures - even to some that are frequently destroyed or neglected - she wiped away the tears from many faces, helping the poor with her savings and the sorrowful with her earnest pity. When the eye saw her it blessed her, for her face was sunshine, her voice was melody, and her heart was sympathy.

This grave was made for her and for himself by Charles Reade, whose wise counselor, loyal ally, and bosom friend she was for twenty-four years, and who mourns her all his days.

www.ingramcontent.com/pod-product-compliance
Lightning Source LLC
Chambersburg PA
CBHW032006040426
42448CB00006B/510